MATT AND TOM OLDFIELD

ULTIMATE
FOOTBALL HEROES

RASHFORD

FROM THE PLAYGROUND
TO THE PITCH

DINO

First published in the UK in 2020 by Dino Books,
an imprint of Bonnier Books UK,
The Plaza, 535 King's Road, London SW10 0SZ
Owned by Bonnier Books,
Sveavägen 56, Stockholm, Sweden

🐦 @dinobooks
🐦 @footieheroesbks
heroesfootball.com
www.bonnierbooks.co.uk

Design by www.envydesign.co.uk

Paperback ISBN: 9781789462340
E-book ISBN: 9781789462357

British Library Cataloguing-in-Publication Data:
A catalogue record for this book is available from the British Library.

Printed and bound in Great Britain by Clays Ltd, Elcograf S.p.A.

3 5 7 9 10 8 6 4

MIX
Paper from
responsible sources
FSC® C018072

For Dylan – a current and future superstar.

Matt Oldfield delivers sports writing workshops in schools, and is the author of *Unbelievable Football* and *Johnny Ball: Accidental Football Genius*. Tom Oldfield is a freelance sports writer and the author of biographies on Cristiano Ronaldo, Arsène Wenger and Rafael Nadal.

Cover illustration by Dan Leydon
To learn more about Dan visit danleydon.com
To purchase his artwork visit etsy.com/shop/footynews

TABLE OF CONTENTS

ACKNOWLEDGEMENTS

First of all, I'd like to thank Bonnier Books UK – and particularly my editor Laura Pollard – for supporting me throughout and for running the ever-expanding UFH ship so smoothly. Writing stories for the next generation of football fans is both an honour and a pleasure.

I wouldn't be doing this if it wasn't for my brother Tom. I owe him so much and I'm very grateful for his belief in me as an author. I feel like Robin setting out on a solo career after a great partnership with Batman. I hope I do him (Tom, not Batman) justice with these new books.

Next up, I want to thank my friends for keeping

me sane during long hours in front of the laptop.
Pang, Will, Mills, Doug, John, Charlie – the laughs
and the cups of coffee are always appreciated.

I've already thanked my brother but I'm also very
grateful to the rest of my family, especially Melissa,
Noah, and of course Mum and Dad. To my parents,
I owe my biggest passions: football and books.
They're a real inspiration for everything I do.

Finally, I couldn't have done this without Iona's
encouragement and understanding during long,
work-filled weekends. Much love to you.

CHAPTER 1

UNITED'S PENALTY KING IN PARIS

6 March 2019, Parc des Princes, Paris

'A dreadful night for Manchester United' – that's what the newspapers said after PSG's simple first leg win at Old Trafford. 'They'll need a miraculous comeback now to keep their Champions League campaign alive.'

Not only were United 2–0 down as they travelled to Paris, but they were also missing three of their most important attackers. Anthony Martial and Jesse Lingard had both picked up injuries, while Paul Pogba had been given a red card.

What a disaster! That only left the manager, Ole

Gunnar Solskjær, with two fit and available forwards: Romelu Lukaku and United's local boy wonder, Marcus Rashford.

If anyone could save the day with a moment or two of magic, it was Marcus. He had done it many times before for United in the Europa League, starting at the age of only eighteen, so why couldn't he now do the same in the Champions League?

Marcus was ready to step up and shine. Under United's new manager, he had found his scoring form again, with seven goals already. In the Premier League, the FA Cup – now the Champions League would be next.

'Let's do this!' he told Romelu as they took up their positions on the pitch.

Although Marcus sounded as confident as ever, he knew that it wouldn't be easy. Even without Neymar Jr, the PSG team was still packed full of world-class talent: Gianluigi Buffon, Thiago Silva, Dani Alves, Marco Verratti, ex-United man Ángel Di María and, of course, Kylian Mbappé.

Back in 2017, Mbappé had beaten Marcus to win

the Golden Boy award for the best young player in
Europe. Since then, he had also won two French
league titles and the World Cup with France, as well
as scoring his team's second goal at Old Trafford.
Now, it was time for Marcus – and United – to
bounce back.

As soon as the match kicked off, Marcus was
racing around causing problems for the PSG defence.
When Thilo Kehrer saw United's speedy Number
10 sprinting towards him, he panicked. His pass fell
between Buffon and Thiago Silva, perfect for Romelu
to intercept. *GOAL – 1–0!*

'Come on!' United's star strikeforce celebrated
together.

Minutes later, Marcus used his pace and power
to beat Kehrer to the ball and then tried to cross it
to Romelu.

'Unlucky!' Solskjær clapped and cheered on the
sidelines. 'Keep going!'

Again and again, Marcus was making Kehrer look
like a fool, but unless it led to a goal, it wouldn't
really matter. And when PSG equalised, that meant

United now needed to score three to win...

Marcus wasn't giving up, though. As he dribbled into the penalty area, he could hear Romelu calling for it in the middle. Cross or shoot? Cross or shoot? In the end, he couldn't make up his mind and got it all wrong. His mixture of cross and shoot curled well wide of the far post.

'Hey, I was here!' Romelu cried out near the penalty spot. He wasn't happy with his strike partner.

So the next time Marcus got the ball, he made up his mind straight away. Even though he was a long way from goal, he was going to shoot. BANG! He put so much whip and dip and swerve on the ball that it squirmed out of Buffon's gloves. And Romelu reacted first to pounce on the rebound. *GOAL – 2–1!*

'Nice one, Rash!' he high-fived Marcus as they ran back for the restart.

One more – that was all United needed now to pull off a miraculous Champions League comeback. Twice Marcus thought that he was through on goal, but both times the linesman's flag went up at the last second. *Offside!*

'Arghh!' he kicked the air in frustration. Time was running out.

And with ten minutes to go, it looked like Mbappé was about to end United's hopes. As he controlled the ball on the edge of the box, he only had David de Gea to beat, but somehow, he stumbled and fell.

Phew! Marcus breathed a big sigh of relief and then refocused his mind. The comeback was still on for United, if only they could create one last chance...

As Diogo Dalot ran forward from right-back, Marcus and Romelu were both in the box, hoping for a dangerous cross. Instead, the Portuguese defender went for goal. His shot deflected off a PSG player and flew high and wide. 'At least we've got a corner,' Marcus thought to himself, but Diogo thought differently.

'Penalty!' he screamed, pointing at his arm. 'Handball!'

Really? After a long and agonising wait while the referee checked VAR, at last it was given – a last-minute penalty for United!

Wow, it was a harsh call, but Marcus wasn't

complaining. Now it was his responsibility to step up and score to send United into the Champions League quarter-finals. As the PSG players protested, he tried his best to stay calm and focused. Put the ball in the net – that was all he had to do.

Marcus had been in high pressure positions like this before, most recently at the 2018 World Cup with England. He had scored in the shoot-out against Colombia; and now he had to do it again.

When the referee blew his whistle, Marcus started his well-practised penalty routine:

Four little shuffles to the left,
then short steps forward to try to fool the keeper,
and then *BANG!*

Buffon did dive the right way, but he had no chance of stopping it. Marcus had struck his penalty with way too much power; it was simply unstoppable.

*Goooooooooooooooooooooaaaaaaaaaaaaaaaaalllllllllllll
lllllllllllllll!!!!!!!!!!!!!!!!!!!!!*

'What a penalty!' Diogo shouted as he chased

Marcus over to the fans by the corner flag. Their comeback was complete.

And what a night. Marcus Rashford: Manchester United Champions League Hero was just the latest step in his amazing football journey. A journey that had started eighteen years earlier in his family's front garden.

CHAPTER 2

FRONT-GARDEN
FOOTBALL

From the very first time he saw it on TV, Marcus was mesmerised by football. As a baby in his mother's arms, he stared at the figures on the screen, wearing their red shirts and white shorts, running around a big green space, and kicking a small white round object. What was this weird and wonderful thing?

'Look Mum, he loves Manchester United already!' Marcus' big brother Dwaine cried out cheerfully.

Melanie smiled and held her youngest son up high like a trophy. 'That's my boy!' she said, looking lovingly at his happy little face.

The Rashfords lived in Wythenshawe, which was proud Manchester United territory, especially in the late 1990s. While their local rivals, Manchester City, were battling down in the second division, United were lifting the Premier League title for the fifth time, plus the FA Cup and the UEFA Champions League.

'I can't believe we won The Treble,' Dwaine marvelled, almost as if he had been one of the players out there on the pitch. 'What a club. What a season!'

United were the greatest team in England, and also the greatest team in the whole wide world. Well, according to Dwaine and Dane, anyway, and Marcus always believed his brothers.

They were his heroes, and as soon as he could walk, Marcus followed them around as much as he could. But there was one place where his mum wouldn't let him go – outside.

'See ya later, lil' man!' His brothers waved, closing the front door behind them.

Where were they going, and why couldn't he go with them? Marcus had spotted the football in Dwaine's hands. It looked like it came from that weird and wonderful game they had watched together on TV.

'Hey, wait for me – I want to play too!' Marcus decided, and he waddled over to the front door to follow them. But as hard as he tried, it wouldn't open.

'Woah, where do you think you're going?' Melanie appeared, scooping him up into her arms. 'Are you trying to escape again, Mister? Look, we can watch your brothers from the window...'

Dwaine and Dane hadn't gone far; they were just having a kickaround with their friends in the small front garden. While they showed off all their tricks and flicks, Marcus stared and stared, as if the living room window was another TV screen.

Front-garden football looked like so much fun! He couldn't wait for the day when he would be allowed to join in. But when would that be?

'Please!' he begged his brothers after his third birthday. They had been teaching him to kick and control the ball in the kitchen while their mum was out, but now he was ready to show off his skills *outside*.

But Dwaine and Dane both shook their heads.

'Sorry Marcus, not yet – you're still too young to play with us big boys. Maybe next time, yeah?'

However, when the next time arrived, their answer was still no. And the next time, and the next time… It was so unfair – he was nearly four years old now! So why couldn't he just join in for a little bit of front-garden football? Marcus was willing to do anything, even go in goal if he had to.

'Fine, you can play,' Dwaine gave in eventually, 'but no crying to Mum if you get hurt, okay?'

'Okay!'

And so, at last, Marcus's front garden football career began.

At first, it was all a bit overwhelming for him. His brothers and their friends towered over him and charged around him like wild horses on that small square of grass. It was as if Marcus wasn't even there. Or as if he were an obstacle that was in the way.

'Watch out!' the big boys warned, nearly knocking him to the floor.

Marcus moved out of their path, but he didn't

walk away. This was front-garden football; he just needed a moment to get used to it.

'Over here – pass!' he desperately wanted to shout, but he was too shy to say it out loud. Plus, Marcus knew that if he did anything annoying, his brothers would send him back inside straight away. He really didn't want that.

'But at this rate, they're never going to give me a turn!' Marcus moaned to himself. He didn't give up, though. He soon swapped his gloomy frown for a fired-up glare. 'If I want that ball, then I'm going to have to win it for myself!'

Marcus would just have to be brave amongst the big boys. With a bold dart, he snatched the ball from under Dwaine's foot.

'Hey!' he complained. 'What are you playing at, bro?'

'It's my turn,' Marcus replied determinedly.

Right, now what? He had the ball, but if he didn't do something quickly, one of the big boys would steal it back. Marcus tried to remember some of the skills that he had watched them do through the window. This was his chance to show that he could do them too.

Flick! with his right foot,

Flick! with his left foot,

Flick! with his right knee,

Flick! with his left knee,

Flick pass! with his right heel, back to his brother.

'Not bad,' even Dwaine had to admit.

After that, the big boys changed their minds about Marcus. It turned out that he wasn't just an annoying little boy who was getting in the way; he was a talented young footballer, just like the rest of them.

'Here you go, Marcus – let's see what you've got!'

Soon, he was allowed to go with his brothers to the local Mersey Bank Playing Fields, although 'only to watch'. But while Dwaine and Dane were playing big eleven-a-side matches with their mates, Marcus practised his ball skills on his own on the sidelines, preparing for the day when he would be old enough to join a football team too.

CHAPTER 3

FLETCHER MOSS RANGERS

The Rashford family didn't have a lot of money, but they managed to find enough for young Marcus to go to football training. After all, it was his favourite thing in the whole wide world, and he was clearly very talented too.

'Good luck, son!' Melanie said, giving her youngest son a kiss. She had to go to work, so Dwaine would be taking Marcus along instead.

'Thanks, Mum!' he replied, buzzing with excitement.

Now that he was five, Marcus was old enough to join a local football club called Fletcher Moss Rangers. But first, he had to prove that he was good enough to play for one of Manchester's top youth teams. Wes Brown, the United defender, had started at Fletcher Moss, and now the club had a strong reputation for developing top young players.

'Top young players like me!' Marcus thought to himself on the way to the Mersey Bank Playing Fields.

He couldn't wait to get started. As his boots sank into the bobbly grass, it felt like he was taking the first step on a grand football journey. First, Fletcher Moss Rangers, then Manchester United and England, just like Wes Brown.

'Welcome, Marcus,' the coach, Mark Gaynord said, shaking his hand. 'I hope you're ready to have some fun today!'

Marcus nodded shyly, as a smile spread across his face.

'Great, then let's get started!'

Dwaine had played enough front-garden football with his brother to know that he was a promising young player, but he was curious to see how Marcus would compare against other kids his own age. It didn't take Dwaine long to see that his brother stood out high above the rest.

And the Fletcher Moss coaches saw it too. From the moment that Marcus first touched the ball, Gaynord could see that he had a natural gift for the game. It was as if he came alive with a football at his feet, his whole body suddenly working in smooth, skilful motion.

The head up, turning, looking out for defenders to beat and teammates to pass to.

The arms out, offering balance through all the twists and turns of the dribble.

The legs pumping, driving him goalwards at top speed.

The feet dancing, moving the ball with such grace and ease until at last, BANG!

Goooooooooooooooooooooaaaaaaaaaaaaaaaaalllllllllllll lllllllllllllll!!!!!!!!!!!!!!!!!!!

Gaynord had coached many talented kids before, but no-one quite like Marcus. 'That boy is a superstar in the making,' the Fletcher Moss coach told himself, and he didn't doubt that for a second. The kid's ability was astonishing. Marcus had already mastered so many tricks and flicks at the age of five!

'How did he learn to dribble like that?' Gaynord asked Dwaine in awe.

'He probably saw me doing it in the park!' his brother said with a cheeky smile and then shrugged. 'Or maybe it was on FIFA, actually...'

Marcus just seemed to soak up football skills like a sponge, whether he was watching his heroes on TV, playing video games, or playing for Fletcher Moss Rangers in real life.

'That's it, yes – brilliant!'

As Marcus's coach, Gaynord soon gave up on teaching him the basics; he was already too good for that. Instead, he focused on finding ways to stop his young superstar in the making from getting bored because even in their twenty-minute matches, Marcus was scoring goal after goal after goal. Often, it looked more like a one-boy skill show than an actual football match.

'Okay, that's enough,' Gaynord would call out when the scoreline was starting to get embarrassing. 'Give some of the others a chance!'

At that stage, Marcus would drop deeper and

switch to setting up his teammates with assist after assist after assist. The Fletcher Moss coach felt sorry for the other teams they faced; they simply didn't stand a chance.

So, how could Gaynord help Marcus to become even better? By setting him new skills challenges to complete, the coach decided.

'So, have you been practising that Maradona spin I showed you?' he asked before kick-off.

Marcus had been working on it all week at the Mersey Bank Playing Fields and then back home in the front garden too. But he didn't all say that to his coach; instead, he just nodded calmly and confidently. Gaynord would just have to wait and see…

As soon as he got the ball, Marcus burst forward on the attack. He was over the halfway line and hurtling towards the penalty area when, at last, a defender came across to close him down…

Right, this was it! Usually, Marcus would dribble around his opponents, or just kick it past the defender and use his speed to reach it first. But not this time; no, he had a new trick to try out. Just when it looked like he was going to crash straight into the defender, Marcus dragged the ball back with his right foot, spun his whole body around, and dragged the ball forward with his left foot. *Olé!*

'Maradona Spin!' Gaynord thought to himself, clapping even louder than usual.

Marcus was away, past the first tackle, but there was another one on the way. No problem! He had something extra up his sleeve to add to his coach's challenge. As the second defender slid in, Marcus dragged the ball back behind him and went the other way.

'Cruyff Turn!' Gaynord gasped. It was extraordinary. How had he learnt that trick too?!

The coach looked across at Marcus's mum, who had managed to get the day off work to watch her son play. 'I've never seen a kid that young play like this before,' he admitted with an amazed look still on his face.

Melanie just laughed. 'Oh come on, Mark – you must see little superstars all the time!'

But the Fletcher Moss coach wasn't joking around,

or being dramatic; he was deadly serious. He had been involved in football all his life, so he knew what he was talking about when he said, 'No, honestly, your lad is going to play for Manchester United and England one day.'

CHAPTER 4

A HAT-TRICK FROM A NEW HERO

Marcus had to touch the red plastic seat behind him, just to make sure that it wasn't a dream. Yes, he really was at Old Trafford, about to watch Manchester United play!

'So, what do you think?' Dwaine asked as he lifted his brother up onto the seat so that he could see the huge green space below.

But Marcus didn't reply; he was too busy staring down at the players on the pitch, and spotting all of his heroes:

There was Ryan Giggs – Number 11,

Fletcher Moss's own Wes Brown – Number 24,

Ole Gunnar Solskjær – Number 20,

And their star striker, Ruud van Nistelrooy –
Number 10!

Hopefully, one day, he would be down there
himself, warming up for United.

Even if Marcus had heard Dwaine's question, he
wouldn't have been able to answer it. With so much
to see and soak up, he was lost for words!

And even if he had replied, his big brother probably
wouldn't have heard him anyway. The atmosphere in
the stadium was electric, with the 60,000 United fans
forming a noisy wall of red. Everyone was looking
forward to an exciting European night. Manchester
United were taking on Spanish giants Real Madrid in
the Champions League quarter-finals.

After losing the away leg 3–1, United had lots of
work to do at Old Trafford. But the belief was still
there, buzzing in the Manchester air.

Come On You Reds!

UNI-TED! UNI-TED!

As Marcus looked around and listened, he couldn't
stop smiling. Watching his favourite team live was
even better than he had imagined!

Although it was a great night for Marcus, it turned out to be a bad one for Manchester United. Their defence was destroyed by the best striker in the whole wide world – Ronaldo. Well, that was what Dwaine said, anyway, and after that night, Marcus agreed with his brother.

First, the Brazilian raced away from Rio Ferdinand and fired a swerving, dipping shot past Fabien Barthez. *1–0 to Real Madrid!*

Then he burst between the United centre-backs to get on the end of Roberto Carlos's cross. *2–1 to Real Madrid!*

And finally, he unleashed a long-range shot that rocketed into the top corner. *3–2 to Real Madrid!*

David Beckham came on for United and scored two goals to make it 4–3, but really it was Ronaldo's night. He was the hat-trick hero, and the best player on the pitch. Even the United fans had clapped when he scored that third thunderstrike.

'Fair play,' Marcus heard the supporters around him say. 'He's a class act, that Ronaldo!'

Marcus and Dwaine were both disappointed

that their team had crashed out of the Champions
League, but they returned home with lots of stories
and memories, and a new hero to admire.

'Bro, come and check this out!' Dwaine called out
from the family computer.

Together, they spent many happy hours watching
highlights of Ronaldo on YouTube. It didn't matter
if he was starring for Barcelona, Inter Milan, Real
Madrid, or Brazil. They were hooked. There were
so many videos, so many goals, and – best of all, in
Marcus's opinion – so many skills!

The silky taps of the ball,

the sudden bursts of speed,

the body swerves,

and, of course, the stepovers!

*To the right, to the left, to the right again, then
BANG! – GOAL!*

Marcus was more mesmerised than ever. What a
player! Out on the pitch, Ronaldo always looked so
free – free to try new tricks, free to express himself
and free to entertain. He made football look like so
much fun.

'Let's watch the Lazio video again!' Marcus suggested almost every single night.

That was one of his favourite clips, from the 1998 UEFA Cup Final, when Ronaldo was playing up front for Inter Milan. They won 3–0 and the Brazilian scored a great goal, where he dribbled around the keeper. But that wasn't the part that Marcus really wanted to watch. No, he was much more interested in seeing the skills show.

'This is it... this bit now!' He pointed at the screen, his excitement growing.

Despite having a Lazio defender tackling him from either side, Ronaldo somehow kept hold of the ball, thanks to some really fast and fancy footwork.

Tap, tap, drag-back, turn, then an Elástico to escape...

And with another calm flick of the foot, he passed the ball onto his teammate.

'Unbelievable!' Marcus marvelled. No matter how many times he watched the clip, it just got better and better. Even when they tried to foul him, the Lazio defenders still couldn't stop him.

But how did Ronaldo do it? There was only one way to find out – time to practise! Marcus grabbed his ball and rushed out into the front garden. From now on, he was going to play the game just like his new hero, however long it took him to learn all the skills.

Marcus dribbled down the left wing and into the penalty area...

Stepover to the left, stepover to the right,

Stepover to the left, shift to the right...

BANG! – GOAL!

Marcus was through, one on one with the keeper...

Body swerve to the left,

Body swerve to the right...

Then, with the keeper lying fooled on the floor, he simply had to tap the ball into the empty net. *GOAL!*

'Wow, so where did you learn those new dance moves then?' his Fletcher Moss coach asked when he first showed them off at training.

'From Ronaldo,' Marcus replied proudly. 'He's my new favourite player now!'

CHAPTER 5

BUSY BOY

Word soon spread about the Little Ronaldo starring
up front for Fletcher Moss Under-7s. It wasn't just
his bright yellow shirt that was catching everyone's
eye. When the team won a big tournament in
Manchester, there was a whole crowd of scouts there
to watch Marcus. They came from top clubs all over
the north of England:

Newcastle,

Crewe,

Everton,

Liverpool,

Manchester City...

And, best of all, Manchester United!

So, was Marcus going to become the latest
Fletcher Moss player to move to Old Trafford? The
club's scout was certainly very impressed. The boy
wonder ticked all the right boxes:

✓ Skill
✓ Speed
✓ Good attitude
✓ Good awareness
✓ Great movement

That last one was really important, but luckily,
Marcus was a natural mover, who had also spent
hours watching and then copying his hero, Ronaldo.
So, with or without the ball, he glided across the
grass gracefully, with pace and power. Full marks!

Marcus was delighted when his favourite team
invited him to come and train at their Moss Side
development centre. 'Yes please!' he replied eagerly.

Suddenly, Marcus was a very busy boy, with a full
football schedule:

Training at Liverpool,

Training at Manchester United,

Playing matches for Fletcher Moss Rangers,

Kicking a ball around in the playground at Button Lane Primary School,

Kicking a ball around with his mates at Mersey Bank Playing Fields,

Oh – and a little bit of eating and sleeping in between!

'You must be exhausted after playing all that football,' Gaynord suggested to Marcus at the start of the Fletcher Moss training session.

But it didn't look that way as their young star got the ball and dribbled towards goal at top speed, his body swerving and his feet dancing. It was like there was no end to his energy!

It looked like there was no end to his ability either. The coach could already see that Marcus's time at Liverpool and United was turning him into an even better player. Back at Fletcher Moss, everything was far too easy for him. The other players might as well have been cones for him to dribble through; they had no chance of stopping him. Gaynord knew that it wouldn't be long before the boy left for good.

But where would Marcus go? Such a talented youngster had so many options. With both big Manchester clubs chasing him, he decided to try training at City too.

That might sound like a strange decision for a mad United fan to make, but the Rashford family had just moved to a new house. Their new home was now five miles away from United's training ground, The Cliff, and his mum couldn't drive. City's Platt Lane Complex, on the other hand, was just around the corner.

Platt Lane was so much easier for Marcus to get to, and it helped that Manchester City were desperate to sign him. The club had climbed back up to the Premier League and their manager, Kevin Keegan, was really giving their young players a chance. Shaun Wright-Phillips, Joey Barton, Nedum Onuoha, Stephen Jordan – they had all come through the club's academy and now they were starring for the first team.

'That could be you one day!' the City youth coaches told Marcus.

Although that was an exciting idea, Marcus was still secretly hoping to play for Manchester United one day.

He couldn't sign with any club until his ninth birthday, but as that day grew closer, United upped their efforts. They weren't going to let their local rivals, City, swoop in and steal such a top young talent. No way! There had to be something that they could do to keep Marcus at their club. If he was finding it hard to get to The Cliff, then they would just have to find another way to get him there…

'Of course, no problem,' Dave Horrocks, the Fletcher Moss chairman, said straight away when United asked if he could bring Marcus and his mum along to the club's main training ground.

Horrocks was always happy to help his young players, plus it was an amazing opportunity to visit The Cliff, the place where the famous 'Class of 92' had started their incredible football careers – David Beckham, Ryan Giggs, Paul Scholes, Nicky Butt, and Gary and Phil Neville.

'Are you excited, lad?' Horrocks asked in the car on the way to The Cliff. 'Because I am!'

On the back seat, Marcus nodded and smiled with his usual calm confidence. Yes, it was going to be a test, but a football test, not a maths test! There was nothing for him to worry about. He was excited, and he was ready to make his Manchester United dream come true.

CHAPTER 6

MADE FOR MANCHESTER UNITED

As he walked out onto the training ground pitches, Marcus felt a buzz flow through his body like a bolt of electricity. Mr Horrocks was right; there was definitely something special about this place. This was it – his big moment, training at the home of the mighty Manchester United. He was following in the footsteps of legends like Becks, Giggsy and Scholesy. Unbelievable!

Marcus wasn't letting himself get carried away, though. He knew that he still had a very long way to go if he wanted to one day become a United hero. This was just the start, the first step up from Fletcher Moss.

But it was going to be a very big step all the same – ginormous, in fact. At The Cliff, Marcus would be competing against lots of other amazing young attackers – the best in the city, maybe even the whole country. What if the club's youth coaches didn't think he was good enough? What if they decided not to give him a chance? All he could do was work hard and play his most impressive football.

'You've got this, bro,' Dwaine and Dane had told him before he had left home that morning. They believed in him, which made Marcus believe in himself too.

'Welcome to Manchester United!' the coaches said, shaking his hand and smiling warmly. 'Right, let's get you playing some football...'

Judging by that first training session, Marcus wasn't going anywhere – he was made to play for Manchester United! Their top youth coach, René Meulensteen, really believed in developing each player's individual skills for as long as possible, from the Under-7s all the way up to the first team.

'That's it – one touch to control. Now dribble forward through the cones, moving the ball from foot to foot, keeping it close to your boot... Brilliant, Marcus – well done! Come on lads, the new boy's showing you how it's done!'

It was the perfect environment for Marcus to learn and improve. Because instead of being told to pass the ball every time he touched it, he was encouraged to take his time, be creative and think for himself. What was the best way to get that ball in the net and win the game? He was free to try new tricks, free to express himself and free to entertain, just like his hero, Ronaldo.

'You looked like you were having fun out there today,' Horrocks said on the drive back home.

This time, Marcus didn't just nod and smile. 'Yeah, it was sooooo good!' he replied, the words bursting out of his mouth with joy. 'At first, I thought it was going to be a bit boring, but Coach got us doing all these really fun skills drills, and then we played a match, 5 vs 5, and I scored six goals, and then...'

Melanie was delighted to see her son looking and sounding so happy. After a few weeks of training with both Manchester clubs, Marcus knew, without any doubt, which training programme he preferred.

'I'll become a better footballer at United,' he told Horrocks. 'That's where I want to be.'

His family agreed, and not just because they were United fans. They worried that some other clubs might try to take away Marcus's unique playing style – the body swerves, the bursts of speed, the skills, the stepovers. But United wouldn't. At The Cliff, the coaches would get the best out of his amazing ability and turn him into a top, top player. Yes, Marcus was made for Manchester United.

'Right, United it is then!' Whenever he could, Horrocks drove Marcus to his training sessions at The Cliff. But when he couldn't, the boy had to make the adventure across Manchester with one of his brothers, or even on his own when he was old enough. Struggling with the weight of his heavy kit bag, he took one bus into the city centre and then another out to Salford. After a tough training session and a long bus ride back home, he would crawl into bed, happy but exhausted.

Luckily, that didn't last for too long. By the time Marcus officially joined Manchester United, aged nine, Dwaine had passed his driving test and bought a car to take him to training. Phew!

'Cheers, bro!'

'No problem. You can pay me back for all the petrol when you're earning £50,000 a week!' Dwaine joked.

Now, Marcus was all set to become a superstar in red, bringing goals and glory to Old Trafford. On the very day that he signed for Manchester United, it just so happened that the first team were training there at The Cliff. What were the chances? It was meant to be!

Van Nistelrooy, Solskjær, Scholesy and Giggsy – they were all right there, just a few pitches away, showing Marcus exactly what he was aiming towards.

CHAPTER 7

ROONEY AND THE NEW RONALDO

By the time that Marcus turned ten, however, he had two more Manchester United heroes: Wayne Rooney and the new Ronaldo.

Cristiano was Portuguese rather than Brazilian, and he was a winger rather than a striker, but just like the old(er) Brazilian Ronaldo, he loved to entertain and show off his silky skills. In fact, out on the pitch, Cristiano probably did even more stepovers.

'Woah, look at his legs go!' Marcus marvelled as he watched YouTube videos with his brothers. As he attacked with the ball, Cristiano's feet were a blur of movement, dancing from side to side. It was all too much for the dizzy defenders. GOAL!

Marcus did his best to copy 'Wazza' and Cristiano. As he was a United fan, they would have been his heroes anyway, but it certainly helped that he got to see them up close at The Cliff, working hard and getting better and better. Sometimes, Marcus would sneak into the gym and sit and watch Cristiano practising a certain skill on repeat until he had perfected it – jumping up for headers, taking free kicks. Didn't he get bored of doing the same thing again and again and again? No, because he was so determined to be the best.

That inspired young Marcus to keep practising his own skills as often as possible, whether he was:

Training at the United academy,

Challenging himself against Dwaine and the other big boys,

Playing all day long with mates his own age at the Mersey Bank Playing Fields,

Or even doing keepy-uppies with a tennis ball on the way to school.

Football was Marcus's favourite thing in the world, and with every kick and touch, he was working towards his Manchester United dream.

Just like his new hero, Cristiano – who on first arriving in England in 2003, had played for himself with all those fancy flicks and tricks. But five years later, he was playing for the team instead. His mind was focused on glory, and growing numbers:

Goals per season – 9, 12, 23!

Assists per season – 10, 9, 21!

Trophies – one FA Cup, one League Cup, two Premier League titles...

...and one Champions League?

Manchester United were through to the semi-finals of the 2007–08 tournament, and Marcus, like most United fans, was dreaming of European glory. He had only been two years old when the team won it in 1999, so this one would be extra special for him.

Come On You Reds!

UNI-TED! UNI-TED!

Five years on from the Brazilian Ronaldo's hat-trick hero performance, Marcus was back at Old Trafford to watch another big Champions League night. This time, United were up against the other

Spanish giants, Barcelona, and it was 0–0 going into the second leg. So no away goals scored, but none conceded either.

Come On You Reds!

UNI-TED! UNI-TED!

As the game kicked off, the atmosphere in the stadium was like nothing that Marcus had ever experienced before. It was as if the noise and passion of the fans was a physical force, pushing the United players forward, up the pitch, towards that final...

In the fourteenth minute, the new Ronaldo, Cristiano, dribbled at the Barcelona defence, weaving one way and then the other.

'Go on, go on!' Marcus urged his favourite trickster.

Gianluca Zambrotta did stop Cristiano eventually, but his clearance fell straight to Scholesy, who took one touch and then fired a wonderstrike into the top corner. 1–0 to United!

As the ball hit the back of the net, Old Trafford roared and rocked like it might fall down.

'Come on!' screamed Scholesy, down on the pitch.

And 'Come on!' screamed Marcus, up in the stands.

What a start! The next seventy-six minutes, however, were some of the most nerve-wracking and nail-biting of Marcus's young football life.

Edwin van der Sar saved from Lionel Messi. Yessss!

Ji-sung Park's shot went just wide. Noooo!

Carlos Tevez got past the Barcelona defence, but not past Víctor Valdés in goal. Noooo!

Van der Sar held on to Thierry Henry's header. Yessss!

Marcus kept looking up at the scoreboard, urging the seconds to pass. Surely, it was time for the referee to blow his whistle? At last, Rio Ferdinand headed the ball away to Tevez, who booted it up field... FWEEEEET – it was over!

'Yes, yes, YES!' Marcus yelled, hugging his brothers and anyone else he could find. What a victory – their team was through to another Champions League final!

It was a night that Marcus would never, ever forget. Those exciting European wins were why he was a Manchester United fan, and why one day, he was going to become a Manchester United hero too. Because if it felt that good just being a supporter, how good would it feel to be a player out there at the heart of the action?

Unbelievable – that was the answer! Marcus didn't really need any extra motivation, but it didn't hurt.

Three weeks later, things got even better. In the final in Moscow, United beat Chelsea 6–5 on penalties. It was another nail-biter for Marcus and his family but at least the right team had won in the end.

'*Campeones, Campeones, Olé! Olé! Olé!*' Marcus celebrated at home with his family.

United were the Champions of Europe, as well as the Champions of England! Marcus felt so proud to be a part of the club, and hopefully, its bright future. He vowed that, after Rooney and Ronaldo, there would be Rashford.

CHAPTER 8

GROWING UP FAST

One day at school, Marcus was asked to write about his dreams for the future. 'Easy!' he thought, picking up his pen. This was his favourite kind of classwork.

'I have one aim in life and that is to be a professional footballer, and hopefully at Manchester United.'

That was it; he wanted to make his family proud and make Old Trafford roar and rock.

As Marcus looked down at the words he'd written on the page, his goal suddenly seemed so simple. But actually, it was anything but simple. He was just one of millions of football-mad kids all over the world with exactly the same aim.

Marcus, however, had two key strengths

that helped him to stand out from the crowd at
Manchester United:

1) talent

and

2) determination

As he progressed through the club's academy,
Marcus stayed humble and Marcus stayed hungry.
Whether it was free kicks or his left foot, there
was always something that he wanted to improve,
something that he wanted to work hard on.

'Come on, time to go home, lad,' the United youth
coaches would tell him. 'We can practise that again
next week.'

It was Marcus's attitude that impressed the club
the most. That was why they decided to make him
their youngest ever Schoolboy Scholar, at the age of
just eleven.

'Wow, thanks!' was Marcus's first reaction when
the coaches told him, but that was before he started
thinking. Wait a second – what did becoming a
'Schoolboy Scholar' actually mean?

Well, the good news was that Marcus would get to

play a lot more football, even during school-time.

'Great, I'm in!'

But the bad news was that, in order to become
a Manchester United Schoolboy Scholar, he would
have to move schools and, more significantly, move
away from home.

'Why?' he asked in surprise. He was only eleven!
'We don't live that far away, and Dwaine can just
drive me there every day!'

Marcus wasn't sure that he was ready to leave his
friends and family behind. Who would he have a
kickaround with now? Where would he live – with
strangers? And would he have to cook his own meals?

'No, there's a nice lady called Maria,' his mum
explained, 'who has looked after lots of young
Manchester United stars. You would be living with
her, but don't worry, we will still see you all the time!'

Okay – if that's what it would take to achieve his
one aim in life, then Marcus would do it. He was
determined.

'Are you sure this is what you want?' his mum
asked, as they arrived at Maria's house for a visit.

It was a big decision and Melanie couldn't help worrying about her little boy. After all, he was incredibly young to be away from home. But if this was what Marcus really wanted, then she wouldn't stand in his way.

By the end of the visit, she did feel a bit better about things. Maria was kind and friendly, telling stories about other Manchester United stars as she gave them a tour of the house.

'Gerard Piqué – yes, he could cause a bit of trouble, but bless him, he's a good boy really. He's gone back to Barcelona now, I hear...'

And for Melanie, it was also nice to know that her son wouldn't be staying there alone. There was another academy star living there too, another tricky winger in fact, called Tom Lawrence. He was three years older than Marcus, but they seemed to get on well straight away.

'Stick with me, mate,' Tom told him with a smile, 'and you'll be playing with the big boys in no time!'

Marcus loved the sound of that. Growing up with two big brothers, he was used to challenging himself against older, stronger, better players. And at the United academy, there were lots of those, especially in the Under-18s team.

Paul Pogba was a tall, talented midfielder from France,

Ravel Morrison was one of the most skilful players that Marcus had ever seen,

and Jesse Lingard was a lively little midfielder with an eye for goal.

Despite the big age difference, Marcus became friends with them. He was mature beyond his years and he wasn't afraid to introduce himself.

'Hi, is it true you used to play for Fletcher Moss?' he asked confidently.

Jesse smiled. 'Yeah, but only for a bit.'

'Cool, me too!' Marcus replied proudly.

It wasn't long until Manchester United's big boys were inviting him to join them in 'The Cage'. That's what they called their exciting freestyle football matches at the club's training centre in Carrington.

Paul McGuinness, their youth coach, thought it was a great idea.

'Just go a bit easy on him, okay?' he warned the older players. 'Remember – he's only twelve!'

McGuinness had a different message for Marcus, though. 'Show them what you can do, kid!' he said with a cheeky wink.

Sometimes, 'The Cage' was 11 vs 11, or even 13 vs 13, with chaos everywhere, and no space to take your time and think. Everything had to be done at super-speed – the skills, the shots, and most of all, the decision-making. Otherwise...

'Too late!' McGuinness would shout from the sideline. 'You need to play that pass earlier there, kid!'

'Yes, Coach!' Marcus would shout back, chasing after the ball again.

He was learning so much, with every minute that he played on the pitch. United's youngest-ever Schoolboy Scholar was growing up fast.

Sometimes, 'The Cage' was 7 vs 7, or 8 vs 8, which Marcus found way more fun. In those games, he had the time and space to really express himself, especially alongside such talented teammates. They made everything look so easy.

'Yes!' Paul called out for the ball.

As he played the pass, Marcus was already on the run again, demanding the ball back: 'One-two!'

When it arrived, he skipped past one tackle with a Ronaldo drop of the shoulder, then played another one-two with Paul. From the edge of the 'D', Marcus fired a fierce, low shot into the bottom corner.

GOAL!

'Yes, mate!' Paul cheered as they celebrated with their special handshake.

On the sidelines, McGuinness clapped and smiled. The future of Manchester United looked very bright indeed.

CHAPTER 9

SIZE, STRENGTH AND SPEED

While Marcus seemed to be on a fast track to the top, he knew that in football, everything can change in an instant. One day, you could be the next big thing and a few weeks later, you could be the next one out the door. Marcus had seen it before. Between the ages of twelve and fourteen, many of his friends had left the Manchester United academy, for all kinds of reasons:

Too small,

Too slow,

Bad attitude,

Just not quite talented enough.

'Good luck!' they told him, moving on with no hard feelings.

For Marcus, it was always sad to say goodbye to teammates that he had played with for years. And it was also worrying – what if he was the next one to go?

But still, Marcus was determined to stay and become a Manchester United hero, even if that dream was starting to look more and more difficult. No-one doubted that he had the skill to succeed, and the willpower too, but what about the size, the strength and the speed?

Speed? Yes, speed! Before, Marcus had been one of the fastest players in the United youth team, but when his legs began to grow, his body struggled to keep up. As it tried to adapt, there was pain and there were problems slowing him down. Suddenly, he couldn't glide gracefully past defenders anymore. But why not? What was going on? It was like he had lost his football superpower.

'My career is over!' Marcus moaned dramatically as he trudged off the pitch after another frustrating performance. He was finding it hard to get into the game, and when he did, none of his skills seemed to work as well as they used to.

There was no way that he was going to become a top winger at United if he didn't retain his blistering pace. Perhaps he would have to move to a different position on the pitch, a position where speed wasn't so important. Maybe he could become a central midfielder instead, using his creativity and football brain...

No, no, no – United's youth coaches weren't going to let that happen. They knew that Marcus was made to attack.

'Hey, don't worry about your pace at the moment, kid,' the Under-16s boss, Neil Ryan, said, trying to lift his spirits. He had coached so many boys with growing pains before and he knew that the bad times wouldn't last. 'You'll get your speed back soon, I promise, but first, we need to work on your strength.'

Marcus certainly had the mental strength, but not the physical strength yet. Without that, he would never get his burst of speed back and big defenders would keep knocking him off the ball too easily. So, it was time for him to build up his core strength in the gym.

Planks, stomach crunches, bridges, leg raises, sit-ups… It was long, hard, boring work, but luckily for Marcus, his teammate, Axel Tuanzebe, was there to turn everything into a competition.

'Right, first to fifty press-ups wins… GO!'

Axel was already a big, strong defender, but Marcus hated to lose at anything, even press-ups. So their rivalry pushed him to improve. Once he set himself a goal, he would keep working until he achieved it.

'Yes, I finally won!'

Throughout those difficult times, Marcus kept smiling and thinking positively about the future. There was no point moaning or giving up on his dream. He just had to get on with his gym work and pass this test. It was all part of the process, part of his journey to the Premier League.

When Marcus saw other academy stars making it into the Manchester United first team, it inspired him to keep going:

First, Federico Macheda,

Then Danny Welbeck,

Then Tom Cleverley,

And then in 2011, Marcus's mates from 'The Cage' – Paul, Ravel and Jesse.

If they could all do it, then so could he!

Marcus also found extra motivation at the 'Theatre of Dreams'. He was there watching in the Old Trafford crowd when Dimitar Berbatov scored a heroic hat-trick to beat Liverpool 3–2, and when Rooney scored a brilliant bicycle-kick to win the Manchester derby against City.

'That's going to be me one day!' Marcus kept telling himself. That's what he was working towards, and it would all be worth it. He could do this; things were going to get better. Size, strength and speed – he would need all three to become a superstar like his United heroes.

'That's it, kid,' Ryan encouraged him. 'Keep battling for that ball!'

Marcus was a young man on a mission. Day after day, he got a little bit bigger, a little bit stronger, and a little bit faster again.

Just after his fifteenth birthday, he got his first England call-up, to play for the Under-16s in the Victory Shield against Wales. Next to Dominic Solanke and Joe Gomez, Marcus looked so tiny, but he didn't let that stop him.

'Well done, kid!' Kenny Swain, the manager, congratulated him after a brave and battling performance. Even on a tough night, Marcus had still shown moments of magic, moving so beautifully with the ball. It was easy to see the boy's huge potential, but he still had some developing to do.

By the time he turned sixteen, Marcus had also experienced his first taste of training with the United first team. What an amazing experience it was, to be up close and personal with proper Premier League stars! He barely touched the ball all session, but that didn't matter. What mattered was that he was making progress.

He was far from being the finished footballer yet, but his youth coaches weren't worried about that. They now knew that he had the hunger and determination to overcome any setback. The rest could wait. The club was happy to be patient with Marcus as his body grew, because this was a boy who was destined for Manchester United greatness.

CHAPTER 10

FROM NUMBER 10 TO NUMBER 9

Yes, Marcus was destined for Manchester United greatness, but what position would he play? After starting out on the right wing, the academy had moved him all over the attack: left wing, striker, Number 10. So, where would he play his best football?

That was the hot topic amongst the club's youth coaches. They'd had a similar problem a few years earlier with another ex-Fletcher Moss forward: Danny Welbeck. Was he a winger or was he a striker? In the end, they left it too late to decide and they didn't want to make the same mistake with Marcus.

'The kid's got too much talent to just stay up front and shoot,' some argued. 'That's not his style. He wants to be on the ball all the time!'

That was true; Marcus was really enjoying life in the Number 10 playmaker role. Buzzing around behind a striker, he had a lot more space and time to use his number one weapon: skills!

But not all of his coaches saw it that way: 'No, he looks like a classic modern striker to me. He's fast, he's going to be at least six feet tall and he can dribble with the ball too. Surely, he's more Thierry Henry than David Silva, isn't he? There's only one thing missing at the moment – goals.'

Marcus did score goals for the United Under-16s, but to become a top Number 9, he would need to start scoring a lot more often. So it was time for some special striker lessons.

'Instead of dropping deep to collect the ball, we want you racing in behind the defence,' the Under-18s coach, Colin Little, taught him in training. 'It's all about getting yourself in the right position, and then timing your run to perfection. Let's give it a go.'

Marcus loved learning new things, especially when it came to football. So, he practised bursting into the box again and again, from every angle.

'Yes!' he called out, pointing forward to where he wanted the pass to go.

'That's better!' Little encouraged him. 'If you're sprinting onto a through-ball at top speed, no centre-back in the world is going to catch you.'

That was only the first part of the striking process, though. Once Marcus had the ball on the half-turn, he had to learn to be lethal. *TOUCH, BANG!.. GOAL!*

'Don't over-think it when you're in those positions,' Little told him. 'It's all about instinct and finding your rhythm. Just picture the goal, pick your spot and SHOOT!'

Marcus wasn't a natural finisher like van Nistelrooy, but he was always willing to work hard to improve. He read all the guides that his coaches gave him and then asked them lots of questions.

'So, let's say Dev is dribbling down the wing. Should I make a run to the near post, or between the centre-backs?'

'If Axel is looking to play a long ball out from the back, should I move out wide into the channels, or stay in the middle and try to win the flick-on for Callum?'

McGuinness and Little were delighted to see their young star taking striking so seriously.

Marcus also watched hours and hours of highlights from the best strikers in the business: Sergio Agüero at Manchester City, Luis Suárez at Liverpool, and of course, his old United hero, Cristiano Ronaldo at Real Madrid. Just like Marcus, Ronaldo had started out as a skilful playmaker, but he had turned himself into a super striker instead. He had just scored sixty goals in a single season!

Marcus could only dream of getting that many, but it was great to see Cristiano combining skills with goals. Maybe he would enjoy being a top striker, after all! Soon, it was time for him to put his lessons into practice on the pitch. Could Marcus shine as Manchester United's new Number 9?

At the start of the 2014–15 season, his youth coaches made a wise decision. They kept him in the Under-18s squad, rather than sending him up into the Reserves.

He was ready to play at a higher level, but there was no rush for him to compete against big, bruising defenders. Why not let him build up his confidence first, against smaller, less experienced centre-backs?

It took him a few games to get going, but eventually Marcus found his scoring form in the Under-18 Premier League. He finished the season with thirteen goals in twenty-five starts.

'He's really starting to look like a striker now!' McGuinness and Little agreed excitedly.

At the Mercedes-Benz Junior Cup in Berlin, Marcus scored two goals, plus a penalty in the final shoot-out, as Manchester United lifted the trophy.

'Hurraaaaaaaay!'

In the 2015 UEFA Youth League, the coach, Nicky Butt, made Marcus captain. In his first game against PSV Eindhoven, he scored a penalty and then burst into the box to convert Tyler Reid's cross. *One game, two goals!*

And what about the FA Youth Cup? The Class of '92 had won the competition, and so had Paul, Ravel and Jesse in 2011.

Marcus knew that it was the perfect place to make a name for himself. He scored a stunning free kick against Tottenham during his first tournament, and he was an even better striker second time around.

As Callum Whelan collected the ball just inside the QPR half, Marcus was already on the move, between the centre-backs.

'Yes!' he called out, pointing forward to where he wanted the pass to go.

Marcus was through, one on one with the keeper, but as he dropped his shoulder and dribbled around him, the keeper clipped his legs. Penalty!

Marcus picked himself up, and then rushed over to pick up the ball. That spot-kick was his. He was United's Number 9 now, and he was going to score. After a slow run-up, he blasted the ball into the back of the net.

Gooooooooooooooooooooaaaaaaaaaaaaaaaaalllllllllllll llllllllllllll!!!!!!!!!!!!!!!!!!!!!

'Get in!' Marcus was really starting to love that scoring feeling. And with every strike, he was getting closer and closer to his target – the Manchester United first team.

CHAPTER 11

DREAM DEBUT 1

'Today, we had Marcus Rashford on the bench,' Manchester United manager Louis van Gaal told the media after their Premier League match against Watford in November 2015. 'He's a fantastic talent.'

Wow, what a wonderful thing to hear! Marcus didn't make it onto the pitch that time, but still, he got to sit with Sergio Romero, Marcos Rojo and Andreas Pereira on the bench. And best of all, he had his own squad number now – 39. It even had a '9' in it!

That season, United were really struggling for fit strikers. They still had Wayne Rooney, plus Anthony Martial and youngsters James Wilson and Will

Keane, but they were often out ill or injured. So, who else could they call on?

'Me, me – pick me!' Marcus tried to show his manager whenever he got the chance to train with the first team.

After all, van Gaal was famous for giving young players a chance. He had handed Clarence Seedorf, Patrick Kluivert and Edgar Davids their debuts at Ajax, then Xavi, Andrés Iniesta, Carles Puyol and Víctor Valdés their debuts at Barcelona. The Dutchman clearly had a good eye for spotting future superstars, so who had impressed him at Manchester United so far?

The club's youngsters found out the answer in February 2016, when Wayne, James and Will all had to miss United's Europa League second leg against FC Midtjylland. Anthony would start up front, with Jesse and Memphis Depay on the wings, but they'd need some back-up on the bench. So van Gaal decided to include his favourite young striker in the squad.

'Mum, I'm in – I made it!' Marcus shouted proudly into his phone.

He couldn't believe it – what an incredible opportunity for an eighteen-year-old! United were 2–1 down after the first leg in Denmark, so there was a good chance that, in this second leg, Marcus might be needed to help attack later in the second half.

In fact, he was needed a whole lot sooner than that. As the squad warmed up at Old Trafford, one United player pulled up with an injury. It was Anthony. Uh oh, what were they going to do without their top goal scorer? Move Memphis up front and then Juan Mata to the left wing? No, van Gaal wanted to play with a proper striker.

'Rashford, get ready – you're starting!'

Starting? For the Manchester United first team? At Old Trafford? Oh boy, this was *BIG!* It was a good thing that Marcus didn't have much time to think about it. Kick-off was only minutes away.

'Just play your natural game tonight,' van Gaal instructed him. 'Express yourself – show the world what you can do.'

'Mate, you're gonna be great!' Jesse told him in the tunnel.

Marcus nodded. He was a little nervous, of course, but mostly excited. His childhood goal was about to come true. They didn't call it the 'Theatre of Dreams' for nothing! All those striking lessons with Little, all those goals for the Under-18s – they were preparing him for this massive moment. He just had to stay calm out there and make the most of any opportunities that came his way.

'Marcus who?' some of the United supporters asked each other when they saw the final team sheet. But they soon knew all about their new star striker.

In the fifteenth minute, Morgan Schneiderlin dribbled into the Midtjylland box.

'Yes!' Marcus yelled to his left, not afraid to call for the ball. He took one touch to control it, and then thought about the shot straight away. His strike was powerful and on target, but a defender blocked it.

'Good effort!' his United teammates encouraged him. 'Keep going, kid!'

With Old Trafford urging him on, Marcus never stopped moving. Sometimes, he appeared on the left, sometimes on the right, and sometimes in the middle. Midtjylland had no idea how to mark him! When his team had possession, Marcus ran into space to make himself available for the pass. And when they didn't, he chased after the defenders to win the ball back. He wanted it all the time.

From a throw-in, Marcus turned and attacked the penalty area at speed. With a left-foot stepover, he made space for the shot... *BANG!* The ball was travelling towards the bottom corner, but the keeper dived down to push it wide.

'Unlucky!' he heard Jesse clap and cheer.

Marcus was getting closer and closer to a debut goal. He could feel his confidence growing with every touch. He was playing with freedom, like he was just in the park with his mates. He even dared to do a cheeky backheel one-two with Juan. The United fans roared with delight. They loved him already! The tricks didn't always come off, but at least Marcus was brave enough to try.

It was 1–1 at half-time, meaning 3–2 to Midtjylland on aggregate. United needed goals in the second half, and soon.

A cross from the right flew over Memphis's head, but Juan just managed to keep it in. He cut the ball back to the edge of the six-yard box, which seemed to be empty... but wait! Marcus had the speed of thought and the speed of foot to get there in a flash. With a cool side-foot, he passed the ball into the net. 3–3!

Goooooooooooooooooooooaaaaaaaaaaaaaaaallllllllllll lllllllllllllll!!!!!!!!!!!!!!!!!!!!

Old Trafford was rocking, and it was all because of Marcus. What a feeling – words couldn't describe it! He raced over to the corner flag and into the arms of the celebrating fans. Only a few weeks earlier, he had been a Manchester United supporter, just like them. Now, he was also a Manchester United scorer.

'Great stuff, Rash,' the captain, Michael Carrick, congratulated him. 'Right lads, let's get another goal!'

And who was most likely to score it? Marcus, of course. Every time he touched the ball he looked so dangerous.

As Guillermo Varela looked up to cross it in from the right, he saw Marcus with his arm up, waiting in space near the penalty spot. United's Number

39 followed the flight of the ball carefully and then placed his shot past the keeper. 4–3!

Goooooooooooooooooooaaaaaaaaaaaaaaaallllllllllll llllllllllllll!!!!!!!!!!!!!!!!!!!!

Marcus ran over to celebrate with the same supporters again. What a night! Was this really happening? He had imagined his Manchester United debut many times before, but this was way beyond even his wildest dreams.

It was a very special, proud moment, not just for Marcus, but also for his friends, family and for all the coaches who had helped him along the way, from Fletcher Moss Rangers and then through the United youth teams – Gaynord, Horrocks, McGuinness, Ryan, Little. They had all believed in the little boy wonder, and just look at him now!

Although he couldn't quite complete his hat-trick, Marcus was undoubtedly the man of the match. A new United hero had been born – and all because of an injury in the warm-up.

CHAPTER 12

DREAM DEBUT 2

The days of 'Marcus who?' were over. Suddenly, everyone was talking about the eighteen-year-old striker who had just bagged two goals on his Manchester United debut. He was now the club's youngest-ever scorer in Europe, beating the great George Best's record. And it wasn't just the goals; it was also the skill, the speed, the style, the energy. Marcus had already created a buzz of excitement.

So what next for United's new young star? With the pressure on, would he prove to be a one-game wonder like Macheda, or was he the real deal?

It didn't take long for the fans to find out. With United's injury crisis continuing, three days later,

Marcus found himself once again in the starting line-up. This time, he would be making his Premier League debut, against Arsenal. Wow, it was a good thing that he was such a cool, calm character.

'More of the same, yeah Rash?' Jesse joked in the dressing room before kick-off.

Marcus smiled back confidently, 'I'll see what I can do, mate!'

He tried to stay relaxed for as long as possible, but once he heard the passion of the fans and felt his feet touch that Old Trafford pitch, his mind was fully focused. Focused on winning, and hopefully, scoring some more goals.

Come On You Reds!

UNI-TED! UNI-TED!

Right from kick-off, United were the team on top, and once again, their new Number 39 was the player to watch. The Arsenal defence just could not cope with Marcus's speed and movement. When he got the ball and burst between two of them, all they could do was bring him down. *Free kick, just outside the box!*

'That's it, mate!' Memphis shouted. 'Keep running at them – they're scared of you!'

Marcus nodded – dribbling at defenders was what he loved best. But he wasn't all about skills anymore; he was also a goal scorer now. So if Arsenal switched off for even a second, he was ready to pounce like a proper Premier League striker...

In the twenty-ninth minute, Gabriel Paulista got to Guillermo's cross first, but the Arsenal defender couldn't clear it properly. In fact, he passed it straight to Marcus, who had stolen in at the back post. He didn't even take a touch to control it. In a flash, he curled a powerful shot past the keeper and into the top corner. 1–0!

Goooooooooooooooooooooaaaaaaaaaaaaaaaaaalllllllllllll llllllllllllll!!!!!!!!!!!!!!!!!!!

That amazing adrenaline rush again.

'Yes, you hero!' Juan screamed, throwing his arm around Marcus as they ran together towards the corner flag. He was certainly part of the team now.

'What a life-changing three days for Marcus Rashford!' the TV commentator cried out.

Two goals on his United debut, and now one on his Premier League debut too – Marcus was on fire! As he leapt into the air in front of the fans, he didn't think that life could get any better.

But there was more to come. Three minutes later, Jesse chipped a dangerous ball into the Arsenal box, aiming for United's new star striker. Marcus had positioned himself perfectly, just like Little had taught him: in between the centre-backs.

'Go on, kid!' the fans urged, growing more and more excited in their seats.

Marcus still had plenty of work to do, though.

He wasn't the tallest of strikers, but he timed his jump brilliantly, keeping his eyes on the ball floating towards him.

Jesse's cross didn't have that much power on it, but Marcus used his neck muscles to swing his head around and nod it down into the bottom corner. *2–0!*

Goooooooooooooooooooaaaaaaaaaaaaaaaallllllllllll lllllllllllll!!!!!!!!!!!!!!!!!!!!

'You couldn't make this up,' the commentator cried out again in utter disbelief. 'This is truly astonishing!'

'Thanks, mate!' Marcus yelled, racing over to give Jesse a big hug. After scoring all those goals together in 'The Cage' when they were younger, they knew each other well, but it was a dream come true to now be doing it at Old Trafford, and for the first team.

Two games, four goals – and still, United's new star striker wasn't finished. He kept running and fighting and calling for the ball. He wasn't playing for himself; he was playing for his team.

When Arsenal's attacker Mesut Özil whipped the ball into the box, it was Marcus who was back there to clear it away.

And when their keeper Petr Čech received a back pass, it was Marcus who rushed forward to close him down.

Later in the second half, when Marcus found three Arsenal defenders blocking his path in the penalty area, he didn't try to trick his way through. Instead, he took his time, looked up and spotted Ander Herrera running forward, calling for the pass. 3–1!

'Thanks, Rash!' Ander yelled as the United players all celebrated together.

After two goals and one assist in eighty magical minutes, Marcus's day was done. As he walked slowly off the field, every United supporter was up on their feet, applauding and chanting his name.

Rashford! Rashford! Rashford!

It was a very emotional moment for Marcus, but just like when he got the ball in front of goal, he looked so cool about it. Nothing fazed him at all. He just calmly climbed the steps to the subs bench, handing out high-fives on the way to his seat.

Pressure? What pressure? Marcus was loving life in the Manchester United first team. He had the self-belief, and also the talent to back it up.

'In my experience, youngsters often play well in their first match,' van Gaal said afterwards, 'but the second is different. Marcus did well in his second match, so he's a special talent, I think.'

It was clear to van Gaal that Marcus had already proved himself; surely now it was easy for everyone else to see that he was definitely the real deal.

CHAPTER 13

MANCHESTER DERBY MAGIC

After his two dream debuts, Marcus's next games for
Manchester United were underwhelming. His next
five games for the club passed without him scoring a
single goal. Oh dear, was the kid going to be a two-
game wonder, after all?

Of course not! Although he was disappointed,
Marcus didn't let his head drop. He kept working
hard in training and listening to the older teammates
around him.

'Don't worry. At your age, you're going to have
good days and bad days,' Wayne Rooney reassured
him. 'I definitely did, anyway!'

Marcus was glad to hear that, especially from a

And a smarter striker too. He wasn't having much luck on the left against the pace and power of Eliaquim Mangala and Gaël Clichy, so Marcus switched to the other side.

At last, United brought the ball forward, out of their own half. As Morgan Schneiderlin passed it through to Juan, Marcus positioned himself between City's other two defenders: centre-back Martín Demichelis and right-back Bacary Sagna.

This was a key part of United's game plan. If Marcus could just get himself one-on-one with Demichelis, he knew that he could destroy the Argentinian with his speed and skill. The plan had nearly worked the first time, and now Marcus was ready to try again.

Anthony made the run down the wing, to drag Sagna out wide. This was it – United's best opportunity to score.

'Yes!' Marcus called out for the ball. He was feeling even more confident now. It was time to show off those fast feet with a moment of Manchester derby magic.

With his first touch, he controlled it,

With his second, he attacked,

And with his third, he slid the ball through Demichelis' legs.

NUTMEG! Marcus was through, one on one with Joe Hart.

'Go on, go on, go on!' the United fans urged, jumping to their feet.

The pressure was on, but Marcus didn't panic. He wasn't going to waste this huge chance. Everything seemed to slow down around him, but he was in the zone, in total control of the situation. He took his time, picked his spot and then slotted the ball past the City keeper. *1–0!*

Goooooooooooooooooooaaaaaaaaaaaaaaaaallllllllllll llllllllllllll!!!!!!!!!!!!!!!!!!!!

What a cool, calm finish in his first-ever Manchester derby! It was his new favourite goal *EVER.*

'Yesssssssss!' Marcus was bursting with pride as he raced into Anthony's arms. He had done it – he had scored a goal against their greatest rivals, City! Soon, he had Jesse jumping on his back too.

'Mate, that was ice-cold!'

Marcus had scored on his United debut, then on his Premier League debut, and now on his Manchester derby debut. He was a big game player, that was for sure.

The next seventy-five minutes were long and nervy for United, but at least Marcus was out there playing on the pitch, rather than watching from the stands. Could he grab a second goal to make things more comfortable?

Before half-time, Marcus ran onto Morgan's flick and tried to dribble past Demichelis again. Just as he was about to skip past him, the defender cut across him and clipped his legs.

'Penalty!' Marcus cried out as he fell to the floor, and so did every other United player and supporter in the stadium.

The referee, however, shook his head. What?! As Marcus got back up, the City defenders surrounded him, accusing him of diving.

'No way!' he defended himself fiercely. Cheating wasn't his style. 'I'm not a diver!'

The City players were trying to make Marcus lose his temper, but he wasn't falling for that. By the time the game restarted, he was calm and focused again. No problem, he would find another way to win the game for United.

He kept dribbling at Demichelis until eventually City had to take him off early in the second half. It was safer that way; Marcus was causing him too many problems.

United's Number 39 was tireless and fearless; even when Marcus got cramp, he carried on fighting for his team. In the last seconds of the match, he dribbled the ball forward from deep in his own half, all the way up to the corner flag. Mangala did tackle him in the end, but his run had relieved the pressure on the United defence and wasted some valuable time.

'Great work, Rash!' Jesse called out when he caught up with him at last.

At the final whistle, Marcus was exhausted, but also emotional. What a day! He shook his head in disbelief. Unbelievable! The last thing he needed was Jesse jumping on his back again, screaming in his ear:

'Mate, we did it! We won The Derby – Manchester is RED thanks to you!'

Others might have become arrogant at that moment, but not Marcus. He stayed humble and hungry. The next day, he was back at school as normal, studying for his BTEC, as if he hadn't done anything special at all.

CHAPTER 14

TROPHY TIME

Two goals on his United debut, two more on his Premier League debut and now the winner in the Manchester derby – could Marcus's breakthrough season get any better?

Yes, if he could win a team trophy! Wasn't that what every player wanted most of all? United were already out of the League Cup and the Europa League, plus they were down in sixth place in the Premier League. So the only competition left was the FA Cup, which they hadn't lifted for twelve years.

'Come on, let's make that trophy ours!' said the captain, Michael, urging on his teammates. As a club legend, he was used to winning lots of silverware.

United's chances of lifting the FA Cup were
looking good until they drew 1–1 with West Ham
at Old Trafford in the sixth round. Now, they would
need to win the replay at the Boleyn Ground. That
didn't sound too difficult, but other than that famous
Manchester derby victory, United's away form was
awful. Still, with Marcus, Anthony and Jesse all there
in attack, anything could happen…

Early in the second half, Anthony burst forward
with the ball and slipped it through to Marcus on
the edge of the West Ham box. DANGER ALERT!
He had one defender in front of him and three more
chasing from behind, but Marcus had been practising
his best Brazilian Ronaldo impression for years.

Tap, stepover to the left, shift to the right…
BANG! – TOP CORNER!

Goooooooooooooooooooaaaaaaaaaaaaaaaalllllllllllll
lllllllllllll!!!!!!!!!!!!!!!!!!!

'Mate, what a strike!' Anthony congratulated
Marcus with a high-five and a hug.

Together, they were forming a very promising
strike partnership, with so much pace and skill.

It was Anthony who grabbed the winner against Everton in the semis to take United through to the FA Cup Final.

'Get in!' Marcus cheered loudly as the team celebrated in front of the fans at Wembley.

A month later, United were back there at 'The Home of Football' to take on Crystal Palace, and hopefully, to end their season on a high.

For Marcus, it was his first taste of that special Wembley Cup final atmosphere. Wow, what an experience! As the two teams walked out onto the field, they came face-to-face with the sights and sounds of 88,000 supporters.

Come On You Reds!

We all Follow the Palace!

UNI-TED! UNI-TED!

EAG-LES! EAG-LES!

Marcus had already played in the Manchester derby, in European nights at Old Trafford and also away at Anfield, but this felt even bigger. That's because there was a top trophy up for grabs. Winning the FA Cup would be the perfect way to end his exciting first season at United. 'Eighteen games, eight goals and one trophy' – yes, that sounded so much better.

So Marcus started the 2016 FA Cup Final like a hero in a hurry. After a clever one-two with Wayne, he dribbled all the way down the left wing and into the Palace penalty area. He almost escaped past Damien Delaney, but at the last second, the defender cleared the ball out for a corner.

'Come on!' the United fans roared, feeding off the energy of their young striker.

Soon, he was at it again, this time on the right wing. With a clever dummy, Marcus skipped straight past Delaney at the second attempt. As he carried the ball forward, he looked up and spotted Anthony running in at the back post. The cross was good, but the shot was bravely blocked.

'Unlucky!' Michael clapped and cheered from midfield. 'Keep going!'

Unfortunately, those were Manchester United's best moments in a poor first half. They were struggling to find a way past the strong Palace defence. It was going to take a moment of magic, and Marcus looked the most likely player to create it. He felt confident enough to try his full range of tricks, even in a big Wembley final.

Early in the second half, Marcus thought he'd finally managed it. With a classy flick, he slipped the ball through to Marouane Fellaini, who struck it fiercely first time towards the top corner… *BACK OFF THE RIGHT POST!*

'Ohhhhhhhh!' Marcus groaned along with 50,000 others.

Eight minutes later, Anthony's glancing header flew towards the bottom corner… *BACK OFF THE LEFT POST!*

So close again! And that was as close as United got to a goal while Marcus was still on the pitch. In the seventy-third minute, he jumped up for a header and landed awkwardly.

'Argghh!' he cried out, clutching his right knee down on the grass.

Marcus was desperate to carry on playing, but he couldn't. The pain was just too intense. With a sad shake of the head, he hobbled off the pitch and straight down the tunnel to the dressing room.

What a disappointment, especially when he was playing so well in a cup final at Wembley! Five minutes later, things got even worse, when Palace took the lead. Nooooooo!

'Come on, United!' Marcus muttered under his breath as he lay there on the treatment table.

Luckily, his teammates fought back straight away. Marouane chested down Wayne's cross and Juan volleyed it in: 1–1 – back in the game!

The excitement and drama carried on in extra-time. When Chris Smalling was sent off, it didn't look good for United. But five minutes later, their super sub, Jesse, volleyed home the winning goal.

'Get in!' Although it was hard not joining in with the team celebrations, Marcus was so happy for his best mate. After the final whistle, he limped over in his team tracksuit for their special FA Cup Final handshake.

'Yes, JLingz – I knew you'd score today! The tekkers on that strike, eh?'

Together, they climbed the Wembley steps to collect their winners' medals. Then, after a short wait, it was trophy time for United.

'Hurraaaaaaaay!' the whole team cheered as Wayne and Michael lifted the FA Cup high above their heads.

What a day, what a season! Marcus still had to pinch himself sometimes, just to check that he wasn't dreaming. His breakthrough year at United felt too good to be true.

And hopefully, as long as his injury wasn't too serious, his sensational season wasn't over yet. Because even though Marcus hadn't made his England debut yet, the manager, Roy Hodgson, had just named him in his squad for Euro 2016.

CHAPTER 15

EURO 2016

When he first heard the news, Marcus couldn't believe it. 'Me, going to Euro 2016 with England, at the age of eighteen?' he thought to himself. No way, someone must be playing a nasty joke on him. One of his mates? One of his brothers?

But no, it was true, it was really happening! After his amazing first half-season at United, Marcus was about to become an England international, and maybe play for his country at a top tournament. Unbelievable!

'It's mad – I haven't even played for the Under-21s yet!' he told his family, shaking his head with a mixture of disbelief and delight.

Ahead of Euro 2016, everyone knew England's

top three strikers: Wayne Rooney, Harry Kane and
Jamie Vardy. However, in Hodgson's squad, there
was space for four forwards, maybe even five.
So, the national team manager had some difficult
decisions to make. Should he go for an experienced
goal scorer like Jermain Defoe or Daniel Sturridge,
or an exciting young maverick like Marcus?

England had a history of taking their best young
attackers to major tournaments. Wayne had gone to
his first one at the age of eighteen, as had Michael
Owen and Alex Oxlade-Chamberlain, while Theo
Walcott had been picked in the 2006 World Cup
squad at the age of seventeen.

So why shouldn't Marcus be next at Euro 2016?
Some argued that it was too soon for him, but others
could see that he was ready to shine.

'I think Marcus Rashford will go to the Euros,' said
former England striker, Ian Wright. 'He has pace, he
makes super runs and he finishes comfortably: He's
got everything.'

In the end, Hodgson selected Marcus and Daniel in
his first squad of twenty-six, but England would only

be able to take twenty-three players to the tournament. Three would be left behind, but who would they be?

Not Marcus! No, he was determined to impress his national team manager, both on the training field and also in the pre-tournament friendlies.

He didn't play in the 2–1 win over Turkey, but with Daniel injured, Marcus made his England debut against Australia at the Stadium of Light in Sunderland. Right, he thought, time to shine! In the second minute of the match, left-back Ryan Bertrand played the ball up to Marcus, who passed it over to Raheem Sterling on the wing.

'One-two!' Marcus called for it back, in space just inside the penalty area.

Raheem decided to go for the cross instead, but the ball bounced off the Australian defender and looped up in the air...

Marcus was onto it in a flash. As it dropped, he calmly volleyed it past the keeper. *1–0!*

Gooooooooooooaaaaaaaaaaaalllllllllllllllllll!!!!!!!!!!!!!

It was another debut goal for Marcus, and this time for his country. It was unreal – he hadn't even been on the field for three minutes! With his arms out wide, he raced over to the corner flag to celebrate.

'Mate, you've got that magic touch!' Raheem shouted, with a big smile on his face.

Marcus grinned back at his new teammate. Hopefully, Hodgson would see that too.

His dream England debut lasted sixty-three minutes, and before he was subbed off, he also helped set up the second goal for Wayne.

Jordan Henderson's pass was coming straight towards Marcus, but at the last second, he heard a shout from Raheem, who was racing up behind him. So with a drop of the shoulder, he dummied the ball and let it run through to Raheem, who crossed it to Wayne. 2–0!

It was high-fives all round for England's new attack. Surely, Marcus had to go to the Euros now?

'I'd take him,' his United captain, Michael, told the media. 'He brings something different.'

Marcus didn't play at all in their last friendly against Portugal, but when Hodgson selected his final England squad, his name was there on the list.

'Mum, I'm in!' he shouted down the phone. 'I made it – I'm going to France!'

Things were moving so fast for Marcus that he found it hard to take it all in. He had dreamed of playing at the 2018 World Cup and Euro 2020, but never Euro 2016.

'This is crazy!' he thought to himself, as he set off on his latest football adventure.

Marcus knew that he wouldn't be starting for England at the Euros, but hopefully he would at least get the chance to be a super sub once or twice.

He stayed on the bench for the first game against Russia, but in the second against Wales, England were drawing 1–1 with twenty minutes to go.

'Marcus, you're coming on!' one of the coaches called out.

Yes! He raced onto the pitch, ready to become England's super sub. In the end, however, it was Daniel who did that job instead, playing a one-two with Dele Alli and then poking the ball into the bottom corner. *2–1!*

As Marcus celebrated the goal with the others,

he couldn't help wishing that he had been the hero.
Still, the main thing was that England were winning.
He had to be a team player and wait his turn.

'Nice one, Studge!'

Having taken his chance against Wales, Daniel got
to start the last group game, and the Round of 16
game against Iceland. Marcus, meanwhile, watched
most of the match from the bench.

'Come on, England!'

After a confident start, the team totally collapsed.
From 1–0 up, they went 2–1 down, and it was like the
players had forgotten how to pass the ball. What was
going on? If they didn't start playing properly soon,
England were heading for a humiliating early exit.

For Marcus, it was so hard to just sit there and
do nothing. He wanted to help turn things around,
but instead he fidgeted on the bench while Hodgson
brought on Jack Wilshere and then Jamie Vardy…

There were only five minutes left, when Marcus
finally got the call. But that was still enough time for
a few moments of magic. As soon as he got the ball,
he raced up the left wing, past one defender and

then another.

'Go on, go on!' the fans urged him on. It was now or never for England.

Marcus was into the Iceland box, with Harry Kane and Jamie Vardy waiting in the middle, but a defender slid in and poked the ball away.

'Come on!' Marcus wasn't giving up. He grabbed the ball and raced over to take the corner himself. In those last five minutes, he completed three dangerous dribbles, more than any of his teammates had managed during the rest of the match.

'Why wasn't Rashford on from the start?' the fans were left wondering. Unfortunately, it was all too little too late for England; they were heading home in disgrace.

So, would Marcus's experience at Euro 2016 affect his confidence? Not at all! Two months later, he made his debut for the Under-21s against Norway, and by the final whistle, he was an England hat-trick hero, walking off with the match-ball.

Marcus was simply unstoppable! And he was already looking ahead to the 2018 World Cup.

CHAPTER 16

LEARNING (FROM A LEGEND)

Back at Manchester United, there was great excitement about the new 2016–17 season. They not only had a new star manager – José Mourinho – but also four new star signings:

Defender Eric Bailly,

Midfielder Henrikh Mkhitaryan,

Superstar striker Zlatan Ibrahimović,

And Paul Pogba. He was back! Yes, four years after leaving to join Juventus, Marcus's old teammate from 'The Cage' had returned to Old Trafford.

'This is going to be so good!' Jesse predicted.

And Marcus agreed. Over the summer, he had signed a brand-new contract, and moved from Number

39 to Number 19. He was making real progress, so he didn't mind about the extra competition in attack.

As much as he loved starting and scoring for United, Marcus knew that he wasn't ready to be the club's number-one striker. Not yet, anyway. That was too much pressure for an eighteen-year-old who had only recently broken into the first team. But now, with Zlatan there to partner Wayne and be the team's top goal scorer, Marcus had time to keep developing his game.

There was so much to learn from a legend like 'Ibra'. He was one of the best players of all time. Yes, he could seem a little too confident sometimes, but he had the talent and determination to back that up in the big games. He had scored goals everywhere – at Ajax, Juventus, Inter Milan, Barcelona, PSG – and had won tons of trophies too.

It was an amazing opportunity for Marcus to improve as a player and a striker. Each training session was like being back at school. He watched Zlatan as carefully as he could and tried to absorb as much information as possible.

It was Zlatan's mentality and focus that impressed Marcus the most. He had never met anyone who wanted to win as much as Zlatan did. Even in their 'friendly' matches during practice, he charged around the pitch, demanding the ball, and then barking angrily if he didn't get it. He was such a strong character that no-one messed with him, not even Mourinho!

If he ever missed a shot, Zlatan didn't let his head and shoulders drop. No – because he firmly believed that he would score the next one. And off the pitch, he worked so hard to keep himself fit and firing, even in his mid-thirties.

'That's what it takes to stay at the top level,' Zlatan told him one day. 'Especially when José is in charge!'

In the Manchester United first team matches, however, Marcus wasn't getting much game-time at all. He only came on as a second-half sub when United won the Community Shield, and he didn't play at all in their first two Premier League matches.

Oh dear, didn't Mourinho think he was good enough? A new manager was like a new start; Marcus would just have to prove himself all over again.

Away at Hull City, he came off the bench to score a last-minute winner. *GOAL!*

Away at Watford, he played a one-two with Zlatan and then bundled the ball in. *GOAL!*

At home against Leicester City, he converted Juan's cross. *GOAL!*

'That's more like it!' Marcus thought to himself as he raced over to the corner flag to celebrate. No matter what position Mourinho asked him to play, he was going to fight hard for his place in the team.

Marcus had switched from a winger to a striker in the United Under-18s, but now he was back out wide again. The United manager preferred to play Zlatan in the middle, with the other forwards taking it in turns on the wings. Marcus didn't mind, but it did mean that he had more defending to do.

'It's your job to mark the full-back,' Mourinho told him. 'When he goes forward, you track back!'

Sometimes Marcus was on the left and sometimes he was on the right. He had good games and not-so-good games, but they were all part of the learning

process. He wasn't giving up or going out on
loan; no, he would adapt, and he would succeed.
Manchester United was his home and he was
growing into a stronger all-round player.

Marcus's biggest problem during those difficult
months was goals. From October 2016 through to
April 2017, he went twenty Premier League games
without scoring at all. The longer his bad run went
on, the more people talked about it, and the more
pressure he put on himself.

'Nooooo!' Marcus screamed at the sky as he
wasted yet another simple chance. He could imagine
the frustrated look on his manager's face.

What had happened to his finishing? If he didn't
find his scoring touch again soon, Mourinho would
have no choice but to drop him.

United made it back to Wembley for the 2017
EFL Cup Final in February, but Marcus spent most
of the match on the bench. And when he did come
on, he struck his one good chance straight at the
Southampton keeper. Noooo! It was the same old
story, with Zlatan saving the day for United instead.

Marcus was pleased to pick up another winner's medal, but he didn't feel like he fully deserved it. He had lost his magic touch! Oh well, he just had to stay strong and keep believing; that's what he'd learnt from Ibra. This was just another obstacle that he had to overcome.

Away at Sunderland, Marcus came on for Jesse with half an hour to go. United were already 2–0 up against the team in twentieth place. Surely, he wouldn't get a better chance to end his goal drought.

But before he knew it, they were into the last five minutes and Marcus still hadn't even had a shot. 'Noooooooooo!' Was he going to go yet another league game without a goal?

In the very last minute, he raced down the right wing and then passed inside to Zlatan. He thought about shooting himself, but instead, he slipped it back to Marcus, who was now into the penalty area. This was it – his big moment to score.

'Go back to basics' – that's what everyone had told him to do: Zlatan, Mourinho, Wayne, Giggsy. 'Just pick a spot and shoot.' Marcus kept his cool, even as the Sunderland defender slid in to try and tackle him. *BANG!* His shot flew past Jordan Pickford and into the bottom corner.

Goooooooooooooooooooaaaaaaaaaaaaaaaalllllllllllll llllllllllllll!!!!!!!!!!!!!!!!!!

As he got up off the grass, Marcus threw his arms high into the air. Yes, another Premier League goal at last!

'Thanks for passing!' he shouted to Zlatan as they shared a high-five.

'No problem, you needed that. Now you've just got to keep on scoring!'

Zlatan's wise words became even more important a few weeks later, when he injured his knee in the Europa League. Could Marcus step up and be United's match-winner instead?

CHAPTER 17

EUROPEAN GLORY

'Arghhhh!' Zlatan cried out as he collapsed onto the grass in agony.

It was 1–1 in the ninetieth minute of United's Europa League quarter-final second leg against the Belgian club, Anderlecht, and their star striker had just picked up a horrible injury.

After jumping up to win the ball, Zlatan had landed awkwardly, twisting his right knee. Everyone knew that he wasn't the kind of guy who went down easily. Uh oh, what were United going to do without him?

Marcus was already on the pitch, playing on the left wing, but Mourinho decided to move him into the middle. This was his chance to show that he was a top striker who could take over from Zlatan.

'Come on!' the United fans urged him on.

Despite his struggles in the Premier League, Marcus was enjoying a good spell in the Europa League. After all, that was where his United career had started, with those two goals against FC Midtjylland. He loved the competition.

Under Mourinho, Marcus wasn't scoring so often, but he was getting better and better at setting up goals for others:

One for Zlatan against Saint-Étienne,

One for Henrikh in the first leg against Anderlecht,

And another for Henrikh earlier on in the second leg.

He was creating lots of chances for his teammates, but now Marcus needed to be United's main striker. His job in extra-time was to shoot his team into the Europa League semi-finals.

'I can do this,' he told himself, as calm and focused as ever. He knew that he would have to do a lot better than his earlier efforts in the game:

A long-range strike that he dragged well wide,

A left-foot shot that hit the side netting,

And a one-on-one where he took the ball around the keeper, but his touch was too heavy.

'Noooooooooo!' Marcus screamed out in frustration. What was going on? He was normally so good at one-on-ones.

Marcus had to find his shooting boots again, and quickly. Otherwise, United would be out.

Early in the second half of extra-time, Marouane headed the ball down to Marcus just inside the crowded Anderlecht penalty area. What an opportunity! His first touch was beautiful to bring it under control, and his second was even better.

Just as a defender dived in for the block, Marcus dragged the ball back. Cruyff Turn! He was on his weaker left foot now and a little off-balance too, but he still knew exactly where the bottom corner was.

Goooooooooooooooooooooaaaaaaaaaaaaaaaalllllllllllll lllllllllllllll!!!!!!!!!!!!!!!!!!!

It wasn't one of Marcus's best strikes, but it was certainly one of his most important goals. When his team needed him most, he had delivered. United were only thirteen minutes away from the semi-finals now. Looking up at the fans, he leapt high into the air, his fists clenched with passion.

'Come onnnnnnn!' he roared.

Sadly, Zlatan's season was over, which meant that Marcus was now Manchester United's first-choice striker. So, could he lead his club to the Europa League final? Yes!

'Keep a clean sheet and try to get an away goal.' That was Mourinho's plan for the first leg against Celta Vigo. The defence stayed strong, and Marcus did the rest. In the twentieth minute, he curled a powerful shot towards the top corner, but the keeper tipped it past the post. So close!

There was nothing that the keeper could do to stop Marcus's fantastic free kick in the second half, however. From wide on the right, it looked like Daley Blind would cross it in with his left foot, but instead, he dummied it for Marcus. United's striker had won the free kick in the first place, and now he was going to take it himself. With a whip of his right foot, he sent the ball swerving into the far corner of the net. 1–0!

Goooooooooooooooooooaaaaaaaaaaaaaaaaalllllllllllll llllllllllllllll!!!!!!!!!!!!!!!!!!!!!

Job done! And back at Old Trafford, Marcus made sure of the victory with another moment of magic. From the left wing, he swung in a perfect cross for Marouane to head home at the back post. It was 2–0 – and United were into the Europa League Final!

'And we're going to win it!' Marcus and Paul celebrated together.

Their opponents in Athens would be Ajax, one of the best young teams in the world. They had Davinson Sánchez and Matthijs de Ligt at the back, Hakim Ziyech and Davy Klaassen in midfield, and Kasper Dolberg in attack.

United certainly had a lot more experience in their line-up, plus one of the most exciting young strikers on the planet.

Marcus wasn't fazed by a big European final. He had already won twice at Wembley and also played for England at the Euros. So as the two teams walked out onto the pitch, he looked as calmly confident as ever.

United were going to win, and they were determined to win it for Manchester. Just two days earlier, twenty-two people had tragically died following a terrorist attack at an Ariana Grande concert in the city. The local people were still shocked and distraught, but Marcus and his teammates would do their best to bring them back a bit of joy, and a trophy too.

In the sixteenth minute of the game, Marcus played a neat one-two with Juan on the edge of the Ajax box. Patiently, they worked the ball across to Marouane and finally to Paul. *BANG!* His shot took a big deflection off Sánchez, giving the keeper no chance of stopping it. *1–0!*

'Yessss!' Marcus cried out, racing over to celebrate with Paul.

Early in the second half, Henrikh scored a second goal, and Ajax couldn't come back from that. United were the new Europa League Champions! And to make things even better, they would now be playing in the Champions League next season.

'Hurraaaaaaaay!' Marcus hadn't been the hero this time, but he had worked really hard for his team, up front on his own; making runs, battling for the ball, and causing lots of problems for the Ajax centre-backs. This time, in the final, he had definitely played his part.

At the final whistle, Marcus had hugs for everyone: Henrikh, Juan, Jesse, Paul, Daley, Michael, Marouane, his old academy mate Axel... And Zlatan, who had come all the way to Greece to cheer his teammates on to European glory.

'Great game, great win!' he congratulated Marcus.

Later that night, United's two top strikers posed for a photo together with the trophy. On one side, a football legend; on the other, a future superstar.

CHAPTER 18

NEW SEASON, SAME POSITION

With Zlatan out injured for at least another six months, would Marcus be Manchester United's main striker for the start of the 2017–18 season? He looked taller, stronger and better than ever when he returned for pre-season training. He now felt ready for the extra responsibility.

But despite Marcus's key role in their Europa League glory, Mourinho had a different plan. In order to compete for the Premier League title, he wanted a big, reliable, goalscoring Number 9, not an inconsistent but talented teenager who was still growing. So United signed Romelu Lukaku from Everton for £75 million.

For Marcus, that meant new season, same position
– left wing. Oh well – it didn't matter where he
played, just as long as he played. And played well.

Marcus dribbled forward at full speed from deep in
his own half, bursting into the space behind the West
Ham right-back. In a flash, he was almost on the
edge of the penalty area...

'Yes!' Romelu called for it, pointing towards the
gap between the centre-backs. Marcus knew exactly
what kind of pass a striker would want. He delivered
the perfect through-ball for United's new Number 9
to strike first time. *1–0!*

As he raced away to celebrate, Romelu pointed
again, this time at Marcus. 'What a ball!' he cried
out, thanking him with a bear hug.

Marcus was happy to help his teammates, but he
preferred getting the goals himself. Nothing could
beat that buzz. He scored:

One against Leicester City,

One against Stoke City,

One against Basel on his Champions League debut,

And two against Burton Albion in the EFL Cup.

Five goals in five games! It was so far so good for the new season.

With United competing for four trophies, Marcus couldn't play every minute of every match. But whether he started the game, or came on as a super sub, he always did his best to make an impact. He celebrated his twentieth birthday by coming off the bench in the Champions League against Benfica.

'Over here, Rom – pass it!'

After only one minute on the pitch, Marcus was already on the attack, sprinting past the right-back and into the Benfica box. He twisted and turned his way past one defender, then tried to squeeze his way in between two more, until eventually they fouled him. Penalty!

'Nice run, Rash!' Romelu said, helping him back up to his feet.

Marcus was now up to seven goals and five assists for the season, and November hadn't even started yet!

By January, however, his great form had faded, and he found himself back on the bench again. Even when Mourinho gave Romelu a rest, it was Anthony who played up front instead.

And on the left wing? Well, United had just signed Alexis Sánchez from Arsenal. So at most, Marcus was getting fifteen minutes at the end of matches to try to create some magic.

'Now I'm never going to get my form back!' he told his brothers miserably. He needed the rhythm of regular game-time to get his season back on track.

'Hey, just keep working hard,' they tried to reassure him. 'And be patient – remember, you're only twenty!'

Marcus nodded. It was easy to forget sometimes just how young he still was. But by February, he was hardly playing for United. Sometimes, he wasn't even in Mourinho's matchday squad at all.

'Where's Rashford?' the fans wondered when they looked at the team sheet against Newcastle. 'Is he injured?'

It was a tough time for Marcus, but he didn't give up. He was too determined for that. All he needed was one more opportunity…

Away at Crystal Palace in early March, United

were 1–0 down at half-time. What was Mourinho going to do now? Romelu, Jesse and Alexis were already on the pitch, and Anthony was out injured... So the manager took off a midfielder and brought on Marcus.

Wow, a whole forty-five minutes! But things actually got worse before they got better. Early in the second half, Palace scored again from a quick free kick. *2–0!*

Uh oh. United really needed a gamechanger now. Although Marcus didn't get a goal or an assist, he helped to turn things around. With his positive forward runs, he pushed his team further and further up the pitch, in search of goals.

Chris Smalling headed in the first, then Romelu equalised, then Nemanja scored a screamer. What an incredible comeback: 3–2 to United!

After that, Mourinho simply *had* to start Marcus in the next league match: at home against Liverpool. It was one of the biggest rivalries in British football, and a game that United always had to win. But how? Playing on the left wing, Marcus would be up against

Trent Alexander-Arnold, a young right-back who was known for his attacking, rather than his defending.

'Use your speed to get in behind him,' Mourinho told Marcus. 'Go out there and give him the hardest game of his young career!'

'Yes, Boss!'

In the fourteenth minute, David sent a long goal-kick upfield towards Romelu. As he jumped for the ball with Dejan Lovren, Marcus was already on the move behind him, hoping for the flick-on. By the time that Alexander-Arnold saw the danger, it was already too late for Liverpool.

ZOOM! Marcus burst into the box, Cruyff-turned his way onto his right foot and,

BANG! He fired a shot into the far corner. *1–0!*

Goooooooooooooooooooooaaaaaaaaaaaaaaaaalllllllllllll llllllllllllllll!!!!!!!!!!!!!!!!!!!!

As Old Trafford went wild all around him, Marcus raced over to celebrate with the fans. He was one of them, after all.

'Yes Rash, what a strike!' Ashley Young yelled, wrapping him in a tight hug.

Ten minutes later, Marcus did it again. This time, as Romelu and Alexis attacked through the middle, he stayed out wide on the left. Virgil van Dijk eventually tackled Alexis, but the ball bounced out to the edge of the area...

Alexander-Arnold had chased back to help the other defenders, leaving Marcus all alone with the ball travelling towards him. He didn't think; he just hit it, low into the far corner again. *2–0!*

Goooooooooooooooooooooaaaaaaaaaaaaaaaaalllllllllllll llllllllllllll!!!!!!!!!!!!!!!!!!!

With his arms outstretched, Marcus stood by the corner flag and soaked up all the cheers and applause. What a feeling! Scoring two goals against Liverpool was enough to make you a Manchester United hero for life.

The overall season would go down as a disappointing one for Marcus, but with performances like that one, his time would definitely come soon.

CHAPTER 19

2018 WORLD CUP

Gareth Southgate announced his England squad
for the 2018 World Cup with a special video,
where each player's name was revealed one by
one. Raheem Sterling was first, then John Stones,
then Trent Alexander-Arnold...

Eventually, two kids appeared on screen, standing
in a Manchester street. One was wearing a red
England shirt and he turned around to show the
name on the back:

'Marcus... RASHFORD!' they cheered together.
'The boy wonder.'

His Euro 2016 call-up had been a total shock,
but Marcus wasn't surprised to be in the 2018

World Cup squad. He had been playing well for his country for a while now. Even so, it was an amazing moment, and another childhood dream come true.

'After years of you standing on the touch line in the cold and rain, Mum we're off to the World Cup!' he tweeted with a picture of Melanie looking proud.

Marcus had been busy training with United on the morning of the big announcement, but he returned home to find lots of nice messages from his friends and family. He tried to play it cool like usual, but inside he was buzzing with excitement.

'Russia, here we come!' he messaged Jesse.

Would they return home as World Cup heroes? Ahead of the tournament, Southgate had switched the formation from a 4–3–3 to a 3–5–2 with wing-backs. It meant one more player in midfield, and one less player in attack.

That was good news for Jesse, and bad news for Marcus. Harry and Raheem were England's first-choice forwards, but hopefully he could come on and be the super sub. If the team needed someone to make an impact off the bench, then he would be ready and waiting.

Marcus sent out a final 'Pick me!' to Southgate in the team's last friendly against Costa Rica. In the thirteenth minute, he got the ball on the right, with time and space to think. What next? In a flash, he spotted that the keeper had come forward a little, off his goal line.

Some players might have seen it and thought, 'No, not worth trying', but Marcus was confident enough to give anything a go. *BANG!* Before the poor keeper knew what was going on, the ball was dipping and swerving over his head… and into the far corner of the net. *1–0!*

Goooooooooooooooooooooaaaaaaaaaaaaaaaalllllllllllll lllllllllllll!!!!!!!!!!!!!!!!!!!

It was one of his best strikes ever, but Marcus didn't show any emotion. He just threw his arms out and walked away, as if he did that every day. Yes, if England needed a moment of World Cup magic, he would be ready and waiting.

In the first match in Volgograd, against Tunisia, it didn't look like they'd need Marcus at all. Harry scored an early goal and England were cruising, but out of nowhere, Tunisia scored a penalty. Suddenly it was 1–1, and a draw wouldn't do for England.

In the sixty-eighth minute, Marcus came on for Raheem. On his World Cup debut, what could he do to help his country?

'Our passing's too slow,' he signalled to his teammates. 'We've got to move it around more quickly!'

Marcus ran and ran, desperate to do something special. It was only in the final five minutes, however, that he was able to get himself on the ball and into the game. With a burst of speed, he dribbled down the right wing and won another corner for England.

Come on!

Seconds later, as Ruben Loftus-Cheek cut the ball back, Marcus was in space near the penalty spot. Perfect! This was it: his chance to score the winner. But then…

'Leave it!' he heard Jesse shout at the last second.

But when Marcus dummied it, the ball got stuck under Jesse's feet.

'Nooooooo!' Marcus snarled, turning away in anger.

Thankfully, Harry scored a last-minute header to give England the victory. Phew!

'In our first game, it's just good to get the three points,' Marcus told the media afterwards, sounding so mature for his age. 'Now we can relax our way into the tournament.'

In their second group match, even without Marcus on the pitch, England thrashed Panama 6–1. Although he was sad to miss out on such a goal-fest, he did get to start the next match against Marouane's Belgium.

Both nations were already through to the Round of 16, and so the managers rested their stars. But for squad players like Marcus, it was a massive opportunity. Raheem had now gone twenty-two games without a goal for England. Many fans were already calling for Marcus to play instead, so if he could score against Belgium...

Sadly, Marcus failed to take the few chances he got. He curled his first shot way past the post and then missed a crucial one-on-one against Thibaut Courtois.

'Come on, you've got to do better than that!' he shouted at himself.

England lost 1–0, Belgium won the group, and Marcus moved back to the bench. His World Cup, however, wasn't over yet.

In the Round of 16 against Colombia, Southgate brought Marcus on as England's fourth substitute, deep in extra-time. There was one obvious reason for that: PENALTIES! Yes, it looked like they were heading for another horrible shoot-out, and for that, England would need their coolest, calmest players on the pitch.

Nothing fazed Marcus; he was totally fearless. But as he walked forward to take England's second spot-kick, all three penalties so far had been scored. The pressure was on.

'Go on, Rash!' Jordan shouted as he threw the ball to him.

With quick, confident strides, Marcus entered the penalty area and placed it down carefully on the spot. As he stepped back to start his run-up, he fixed his eyes first on the ball and then on the goal in front of him. That helped him to focus and ignore the noise of the crowd.

After four little shuffles to the left, Marcus moved forward, taking short steps to try to fool the keeper. David Ospina did guess the right way, but Marcus tucked the ball right into the bottom corner. *GOAL!*

Ice-cold! He didn't celebrate at all; not even a fist pump. Instead, Marcus jogged over to Jordan to give him some encouragement. It worked. Six spot-kicks later, England had won the shoot-out. They were into the World Cup quarter-finals!

'Yesssssssssss!' Marcus didn't join the big player pile-up, but he stood next to it, smiling. What a moment, what an achievement! He was so proud to be a part of English football history.

And their Russian adventure continued. The quarter-final finished England 2 Sweden 0. Easy! Marcus had only come on for the last minute, but winning was one big squad effort. Everyone could see that, especially the fans back home. They had fallen in love with the national team again.

There were high hopes for the semi-final against

Croatia and it started so well. In the fifth minute, Kieran Trippier curled a free kick into the top corner. 1–0!

'Get in!' Marcus punched the air on the sidelines.

But in the second half, as England tired, Croatia seemed to grow stronger. With twenty minutes to go, Ivan Perišić got the equaliser. *1–1!*

'Marcus, get ready – you're coming on!'

'Yes, Coach!'

With his fast, fresh legs, Marcus was determined to make an impact. He chased after every long punt and pass, putting the Croatian defenders under pressure. If only he could get one good chance…

As the ball dropped, Domagoj Vida missed his header and for a second, it looked like Marcus might be in. But it bounced up over his head and the Croatian keeper rushed out to collect it.

'Ohhhhhhhhh!' groaned every England player and supporter, including Marcus.

He kept chasing everything right until the end of extra-time, but by then, Croatia had scored the winning goal. It was all over, and England were out of the World Cup.

At the final whistle, Marcus collapsed onto the grass, his hands covering the tears streaming down his face. It was a devastating feeling, one of the worst he had ever experienced. He had given absolutely everything, and yet it hadn't been enough.

'Hey, you've been brilliant,' Southgate said, helping him back up. 'You should be so proud of what you've achieved!'

Although his manager was right, it didn't feel that way out there on the pitch in Moscow. It was so disappointing to come so close. As the players stood in front of the fans, thanking them for all their support, Marcus was already thinking ahead to next time.

Next time, he would be starring in the starting line-up.

And next time, he would lead England all the way to the World Cup final.

CHAPTER 20

UNITED'S NEW NUMBER 10

Marcus returned from the 2018 World Cup feeling more determined than ever. He was going to make this his greatest year yet at Old Trafford, the season where he went from inconsistent kid to reliable scorer, from 'Boy Wonder' to 'Star Striker'. It was time. Marcus was nearly twenty-one now, and he was also United's new Number 10.

Wow, what an honour! That shirt had been worn by so many of the club's most famous forwards:

Denis Law,

Mark Hughes,

Teddy Sheringham,

Ruud van Nistelrooy,

And, of course, Wayne Rooney, his hero and mentor.

'It suits you mate,' he wrote on social media when Marcus first wore his old number.

It was one of his proudest moments, especially as a lifelong Manchester United fan. Now, Marcus had to prove himself worthy to wear the shirt. He had scored seven Premier League goals last season and now he was looking to double that, at least.

'Let's do this!' he said with one arm around Romelu and the other around Anthony. They were Numbers 9, 10 and 11 now and between them, they had everything they needed to become one of the best attacking trios in Europe.

The new season didn't start the way Marcus had hoped, however. After a win against Leicester, they lost to Brighton and then, things would get even worse against Burnley, despite a promising start: United were already winning 2–0 when he came on. It should have been a nice, comfortable afternoon, but instead, he surprisingly lost his cool.

As Marcus tried to dribble past Phil Bardsley, the

Burnley right-back kicked the ball out for a corner and then took a second, angry kick at him.

'Hey!' Marcus cried out as he fell to the floor. 'You can't do that!'

When he got back up, Marcus walked over towards Bardsley. He was so furious that he made the mistake of going head-to-head with the defender.

'Ref!' Bardsley called out, touching his head and pretending to be in pain. 'Did you see that?'

The referee ran over and reached into his pocket: RED CARD!

What? Marcus couldn't believe it. At first, he blamed Bardsley and the referee, but once he had calmed down a bit in the dressing room, he realised it was really his own fault. How could he be so stupid? He had fallen for the oldest trick in the book!

'Sorry to everyone at the club and all the fans,' Marcus wrote on Twitter. He had learnt his lesson.

After that bad start to a fresh chapter as United's new Number 10, Marcus soon bounced back. He wasn't yet banging in the goals every game, but he showed flashes of his brilliance. He scored a flick volley against West Ham, he caught the Fulham keeper out at his near post, and he grabbed a last-minute winner away at Bournemouth.

'Come on!' Marcus roared as he raced over to the United fans in the corner. That was more like it; he was scoring goals when his team needed him most.

Although it was an important win, there was still plenty of room for improvement. United were meant to be challenging for the Premier League title, or at least the Top Four, but instead, they were way down in eighth place. That simply wasn't good enough, especially with such a talented and expensive squad.

'We spent £90 million on Pogba – what a waste of money that was!' some supporters moaned. 'And what's happened to Rashford? I thought he was going to be as good as Mbappé!'

All was not well at Old Trafford. In December, the club directors decided that it was time for another fresh start. They were going to replace Mourinho with a new manager, and announced that, until the end of the season, that would be Ole Gunnar Solskjær, the legendary striker who had scored United's winning goal in the 1999 Champions League final.

The atmosphere at the club seemed to change straight away. Suddenly, everyone was excited again:

Ole's at the wheel,
Tell me how does it feel,
We've got Sanchez, Paul Pogba and Fred,
Marcus Rashford, a Manc born and bred,
Duh du, du du du du du
Duh du, du du du du du!

Solskjær was certainly a fans' favourite, but could he really help to turn things around at Old Trafford? As a fellow striker, Marcus had a good feeling about it.

CHAPTER 21

SCORING AGAIN UNDER SOLSKJÆR

Solskjær's first message to the Manchester United players was clear and simple: 'I want us to play forward and I was us to play fast.'

After all, what was the point in having the power of Paul and the pace of Marcus and Anthony in attack if they weren't going to use it properly? The plan was to bring back the style of the United of old, the one that had won so many trophies under Sir Alex Ferguson. That team had been impossible to stop, and also exciting to watch.

'Yeah!' everyone agreed eagerly.

There was lots of work to be done first, however, all over the pitch. As a former striker himself,

Solskjær focused on helping the forwards in particular. He could understand Marcus's amazing potential – his speed, his skill, his strength, his intelligence – but he could also see the weaknesses in his game.

'I want you to be our star striker from now on,' the manager encouraged him. 'I know you can do it, but you need to score more goals. So let's turn you into a clinical finisher!'

Together, they worked hard on Marcus's movement in the box and, most importantly, his composure in front of goal.

'Don't rush the shot!' Solskjær kept telling him. 'Take your time, stay calm and pick your spot. The goal's not going to move!'

Soon, Marcus was ready to put that finishing into practice on the pitch. Meanwhile, Solskjær continued to assemble his squad for his first match as United manager. He picked:

Anthony on the left,

Jesse on the right,

And Marcus in the middle!

Marcus knew his new manager really believed in him, and that gave him a much-needed boost. Now, it was time to say thanks.

In the second minute of the away match against Cardiff City, the opposition gave away a free kick just outside their penalty area. And up stepped Marcus to blast the ball into the bottom corner. *1–0!*

Goooooooooooooooooooooaaaaaaaaaaaaaaaaallllllllllll llllllllllllll!!!!!!!!!!!!!!!!!!!

At the full-time whistle, United were 5–1 winners. What a start!

Marcus was delighted to score another fantastic free kick, but he kept thinking about the one-on-one that he had missed in the second half. Despite staying calm and picking his spot, the Cardiff keeper had deflected his shot wide. Had Marcus rushed his finish again? Should he have aimed for the other side instead?

'Hey, don't worry about it,' Solskjær reassured him. 'You'll score that next time.'

Marcus was a man on a mission. In the fourth minute against Bournemouth, he danced his way through their defence with Ronaldo-esque footwork.

He poked the ball past the first, then did an elástico to escape from the second, before crossing it for Paul to tap in. 1–0!

Marcus had an assist; now he wanted a goal of his own. At the end of the first half, Anthony delivered a deep cross towards the Bournemouth back post. With a burst of speed, Marcus got to it first, stretched out his right boot, and somehow flicked the ball into the opposite corner of the net. *3–0!*

Gooooooooooooooooooooaaaaaaaaaaaaaaaaalllllllllllll lllllllllllllll!!!!!!!!!!!!!!!!!!!!!

With Solskjær's support, Marcus was back to his absolute best, and it was beautiful to watch. He was playing almost every minute of every United match.

Away at Newcastle, Alexis passed it through to Marcus, who was unmarked on the edge of the six-yard box. It was one of those chances that a star striker simply had to score. As the keeper rushed out towards him, Marcus took one touch to control the ball and then calmly placed it past Martin Dúbravka. *2–0!*

Gooooooooooooooooooooaaaaaaaaaaaaaaaaalllllllllllll lllllllllllllll!!!!!!!!!!!!!!!!!!!!!

On the sidelines, Solskjær clapped and smiled. Much better, Marcus!

'He's got frightening pace, he's now become stronger, he can hold the ball up for us and he's a great link player,' the United manager told the media. 'He can become a top, top player.'

Now that Marcus had finally found his striker's rhythm, the goals were flooding in.

Away at Tottenham, Paul spotted Marcus's run and played the perfect long pass. As he reached the ball on the edge of the penalty area, Marcus thought about hitting it first time, but then he heard his manager's voice in his head:

'Don't rush the shot!'

So instead, he took a touch and carefully picked his spot. *BANG!* – bottom corner. *1–0!*

Gooooooooooooooooooooaaaaaaaaaaaaaaaaalllllllllllll llllllllllllll!!!!!!!!!!!!!!!!!!!!

It was a brilliant strike from a very difficult angle, but Marcus made it look so easy. His finishing was improving with every game and every goal.

'Come on!' he shouted, punching the air with

passion. He was getting used to that great goalscoring feeling. He scored the winners for United against Brighton and Leicester City too.

Six goals in eight games! That took him up to nine for the Premier League season, his best-ever total. At last, this was the big breakthrough that Marcus had been working towards; his move from 'Boy Wonder' to 'Star Striker'.

One of his old teammates agreed: 'Rashford is the future of Manchester United,' Zlatan announced. 'Now he is using his quality more for the team, not just for himself. He has big potential – he has no limits.'

In the Champions League, Marcus came face-to-face with Europe's top wonderkid, Kylian Mbappé. Let the battle begin! The Frenchman won the first leg, scoring PSG's second goal at Old Trafford, but it was Marcus who won the second leg in Paris.

First, he hit a long-range rocket that Gianluigi Buffon couldn't hold. Romelu raced in to grab the rebound. *GOAL!*

'Come on, we can do this!' Marcus cheered with confidence.

Then, in the very last minute, just when it looked like it was all over for United, they won a penalty. And after four long minutes of VAR and arguing, it was Marcus who stepped up to take it. It was the biggest moment of his football career, but he was a calm, clinical, world-class finisher now.

Goooooooooooooooooooaaaaaaaaaaaaaaaaalllllllllll llllllllllllll!!!!!!!!!!!!!!!!!!

'Yes, Rash!'

'What a hero!' his teammates cheered as they chased him over to the corner flag.

United were through to the Champions League quarter-finals, thanks to their new star striker.

Unfortunately, their form soon fizzled out after that, but for Marcus, the most important thing was making progress. As a team, they were starting to play more exciting football, and as a striker, he was starting to look like a more lethal finisher. 2018–19 had been his best scoring season so far, and 2019–20 was going to be even better.

CHAPTER 22

FINDING THE NET IN THE NATIONS LEAGUE

Marcus was starting to get more game-time for England too. After the 2018 World Cup, Southgate decided to switch formation again, this time back to a 4–3–3. Suddenly, there was space for three forwards in the team: Raheem, Harry and one more... Marcus!

Although he was the most popular choice, there was plenty of competition: Danny Welbeck, James Maddison, Callum Wilson, and Jadon Sancho, the new boy wonder on the block. Jadon was only eighteen and he was already playing brilliantly on the right wing for Borussia Dortmund in Germany.

'Man, you're making me feel old!' Marcus joked.

He knew that he would need to work hard to secure that starting spot, starting with the UEFA Nations League. It was a brand-new European tournament and England were up against two of the top teams in the world: Spain and their World Cup rivals, Croatia. Wow, it wouldn't be easy, but Marcus always loved a challenge.

'They're going to be really good games for us,' he said in an interview. 'We have to start beating these bigger countries in the world and there's no two better opponents to do that against.'

In order to win, England would need goals, and not just from Harry. So far, Marcus had only scored three international goals in twenty-five appearances. Okay, so he had come off the bench in a lot of those games, but still, it was a disappointing record for someone who was supposed to be a striker. It was time to change that.

At Wembley, England got off to the perfect start against Spain. As Harry spread the ball out to Luke Shaw on the left, Marcus was already in position, between the defenders, and ready to make his move.

'Now!' he called out, bursting into the box.

Luke's pass was perfect and so was Marcus's finish, past their United teammate, David. *1–0!*

Goooooooooooooooooooaaaaaaaaaaaaaaaaalllllllllllll llllllllllllllllll!!!!!!!!!!!!!!!!!!!!!

Marcus didn't race away to celebrate; he jogged. He was Mr Cool, especially in front of goal these days. For United, and now for England too.

Sadly, Spain fought back to win 2–1, but Marcus knew that the team was moving in the right direction. He certainly was. Three days later, in a friendly against Switzerland, he snuck in at the back post to volley home the winner.

'What a finish, Rash!' Danny Rose shouted, giving him a big hug.

Two in two – England had a new star striker now!

Marcus missed a couple of good chances in the disappointing 0–0 draw against Croatia, but he didn't let that get him down. Instead, he looked forward, to England's second game against Spain. It was now a must-win match. Otherwise, they had no chance of making it to the Nations League Finals.

'Come on, we can do this!' Southgate told his team before kick-off.

For Marcus, it felt like a massive moment in his international career. If he failed, Jadon was there, waiting impatiently on the bench, ready to take his place. But if he succeeded...

For the first forty magnificent minutes, England's exciting new front three destroyed the Spanish defence together.

First, Harry passed to Marcus, who delivered a dangerous cross to Raheem. *1–0!*

Then Harry slipped a brilliant pass through to Marcus, who calmly fired a shot into the bottom corner. *2–0!*

And finally, Harry slid the ball across to Raheem in the six-yard box. *3–0!*

'Yesssss!' Marcus punched the air with pride. The England attack was on fire, and they were having so much fun together. Their speed, their skill, their movement and their shooting; they were too hot for even top defenders like Sergio Ramos to handle.

Although Spain fought back in the second half

once again, this time, England held on for a huge
3–2 victory.

'Top work tonight!' Southgate told Marcus with a
smile and hug as the squad celebrated out on the pitch.

'Thanks, Boss!'

Hopefully, with more goals and more performances
like that, Marcus could secure his place alongside
Raheem and Harry in attack.

'Rashford is a tremendous talent,' Southgate
confirmed, just in case anyone still doubted it.

With a 2–1 win over Croatia, England made it
through to the Nations League Finals, where they
faced the Netherlands in the semis. Harry was out
injured, so Marcus was now England's central striker,
up against two of the best defenders in the world:
Virgil van Dijk and Matthijs de Ligt.

'Bring it on!' Marcus had given de Ligt a tough
game in the Europa League final back in 2017; now,
it was time to test him again.

In the thirtieth minute, the Netherlands were
looking very comfortable as they passed the ball
around at the back. But as it came to de Ligt, he lost

his concentration and let it slip under his foot. It was only a half-mistake, but that was all that Marcus needed. In a sprint race, he could beat almost anyone. He got to the ball first, just before de Ligt, who kicked Marcus's shin instead. *Penalty!*

He picked himself up and put the ball down on the spot. Without Harry, Marcus was England's penalty taker now. No problem! After four little shuffles to the left, he moved forward, taking short steps to try to fool the keeper. It worked. As Jasper Cillessen dived to his right, Marcus placed his shot in the opposite corner. *1–0!*

Goooooooooooooooooooaaaaaaaaaaaaaaaaalllllllllllll llllllllllllll!!!!!!!!!!!!!!!!!!

As cool as you like! He jogged over to the England fans, holding up the Three Lions on his shirt. Harry who? Marcus was a top finisher too!

When the second half started, however, he wasn't out there on the pitch. Marcus had tried his best to ignore his injured ankle, but eventually, it was just too painful to play on.

'Good luck, lads!' he told his teammates.

Without Marcus, however, England lost their way. From 1–0 up, they fell to a 3–1 defeat and crashed out of the competition.

It was a disappointing way to end, but overall, Marcus had enjoyed his first Nations League experience. Hopefully his three goals had earned him a regular England starting spot, especially with the next Euros coming up soon.

CHAPTER 23

UNITED'S STAR STRIKER

30 October 2019, Stamford Bridge, London

Almost three months into the new season, and Manchester United were still struggling to find their form. Their new star striker, however, had certainly found his. Marcus's scoring run had started on the opening day with two classy finishes against Chelsea. Now, United were on their way to Stamford Bridge to take on Chelsea again, this time in the Carabao Cup fourth round.

As the team travelled down to London, Marcus had every reason to feel confident. It had been a fantastic week for him. First, he had converted

Daniel James' cross to end Liverpool's seventeen-match winning streak, and then he had calmly slotted home against Norwich City. That was his fifth goal of the season and his fiftieth for United.

Two in two! Even a missed penalty wasn't going to get him down. Harry Kane, Sergio Agüero, Pierre-Emerick Aubameyang, and Marcus Rashford – *that's* where he was aiming to be, amongst the most prolific strikers in the Premier League.

'Yes!' Marcus called out for the ball, as Daniel dribbled up the right wing. He was in space on the edge of the area, in between two Chelsea defenders. Daniel, however, decided to go it alone. He danced his way into the box, where Marcos Alonso brought him down. *Penalty to United!*

'Great work!' Marcus told Daniel, quickly grabbing the ball. He was determined to take it, despite that miss against Norwich.

Marcus went through his usual spot-kick routine, but faster this time, as if he couldn't wait to… SCORE! *1–0!*

Goooooooooooooaaaaaaaaaaaallllllllllllllllllll!!!!!!!!!!!!!!

It was a perfect penalty, sending the keeper the wrong way. As Marcus and his teammates celebrated with cool high-fives, their manager, Solskjær, punched the air with both fists. Thank goodness their star striker was on fire!

United's lead lasted all the way until the sixtieth minute, when Michy Batshuayi scored a superb solo goal. 1–1! Uh oh, the pressure was back on the team in red. They needed something special from their star striker, otherwise their cup run would be over.

In the seventy-second minute, Fred won a free kick for United, thirty-five yards out from the Chelsea goal. It would take a wonderstrike to beat Willy Caballero from there, but Marcus was always up for a challenge.

Although he was getting better and better at scoring tap-ins these days, he still preferred the spectacular long-range rockets he hit like those of Cristiano Ronaldo. Those were the shots that Marcus practised most after training, and they were the goals that he remembered most too. That free kick against Celta Vigo in the Europa League semi-final, that dipping, swerving shot for England versus Costa Rica; those were moments that Marcus would never ever forget.

It was time to add one more to that incredible collection, on the night before his twenty-second birthday. One, two, three steps and then BANG! As soon as the ball left his boot, Marcus knew that it was a good, clean strike. He watched it fly high over the jumping heads in the Chelsea wall…

'Now, down and a little to the left!' Marcus muttered, as if the ball could hear him.

Maybe it could because not only did it dip, but it also swerved, away from Caballero and into the top corner. 2–1!

Gooooooooooooooooooooooaaaaaaaaaaaaaaaalllllllllllllllll lllllllllll!!!!!!!!!!!!!!!!!!!!!

It was a beauty, easily one of the best he had ever scored. What a way to win a match! Marcus raced away to celebrate, sliding on his knees towards the United fans in the corner.

'You hero!' Ashley screamed, hugging him tightly as he got back up to his feet.

'Come on!' Marcus roared over his teammate's shoulder.

There was nothing he loved more than scoring spectacular strikes for his club. Like his hero Cristiano, he was now combining skills with goals. Marcus was so proud to be United's new Number 10, their consistent star striker at last.

After that stunner at Stamford Bridge, the goals kept coming. Now that he had found his rhythm, suddenly Marcus just couldn't stop scoring: against Partizan Belgrade in the Europe League; then back in the Premier League against Brighton, Sheffield United, two against Tottenham, and then one in United's Manchester derby win over City.

Marcus didn't even have to think about it anymore; he just shot and scored. Simple!

He grabbed one against Colchester in the Carabao Cup quarter-finals, then one against Newcastle, one against Burnley, and another two against Norwich.

Wow, it was still only January, and Marcus was already up to nineteen goals for the season! He had well and truly smashed all of his previous scoring records.

'Rashford is really starting to look like the real deal,' one journalist wrote. 'He now deserves to be called world class.'

Nearly four years after his dream debut against FC Midtjylland, Marcus was at last living up to those early expectations. There had been tough times along the way, but he had never stopped believing in himself and his ability. Now, it was official; the boy wonder had become United's star striker.

And a few months later, Marcus made another massive leap, this time from football hero to national hero. Despite all the fame and fortune of playing for Manchester United and England, he had never forgotten his younger years in Wythenshawe. Back then, his mum, Melanie, had worked so hard to put food on the table for the family. And if it weren't for the free meals that he got at school, some days Marcus might have gone hungry.

So when the schools closed during the devastating coronavirus pandemic and those free meals stopped, he knew that he had to do something to help. Once upon a time, he had been one of the children who relied on that food and without it, Marcus might not have gone on to achieve his football dreams. He couldn't just sit back and let those kids go hungry; this was his chance to make a difference, to be a gamechanger off the football pitch, as well as on it.

Teaming up with a charity called FareShare, Marcus helped raise almost £1 million. Wow, that was enough money to provide more than 3 million meals per week to vulnerable children across the country!

'Thank you all SO much for the support,' he tweeted. 'And whilst I'm celebrating this, there is SO much more to do.'

As the summer holidays approached, Marcus stood up and spoke out again, sending a public letter to all the MPs in Parliament.

'Please reconsider your decision to cancel the food voucher scheme,' he wrote with passion and understanding. 'This is England in 2020, and this is an issue that needs urgent assistance.'

Marcus' amazing message spread far and wide

through social media, calling on the Prime Minister, Boris Johnson, to act. And it worked! Just one day after his letter, the government announced a new summer food fund for vulnerable children, worth over £120 million.

Although Marcus was the hero of the hour, he was too humble to take the credit.

'Just look at what we can do when we come together,' he told his fans. 'THIS is England in 2020.'

Manchester United

🏆 FA Cup: 2015–16

🏆 League Cup: 2016–17

🏆 UEFA Europa League: 2016–17

Individual

🏆 Manchester United Young Player of the Year: 2015–16

🏆 Premier League Player of the Month: January 2019

RASHFORD

10

THE FACTS

NAME: Marcus Rashford

DATE OF BIRTH: 31 October 1997

AGE: 23

PLACE OF BIRTH: Wythenshawe, Manchester

NATIONALITY: England

BEST FRIEND: Jesse Lingard

CURRENT CLUB: Manchester United

POSITION: ST

THE STATS

Height (cm):	**185**
Club appearances:	**240**
Club goals:	**79**
Club trophies:	**4**
International appearances:	**39**
International goals:	**11**
International trophies:	**0**
Ballon d'Ors:	**0**

★ ★ ★ **HERO RATING: 86** ★ ★ ★

GREATEST MOMENTS

25 FEBRUARY 2016, MANCHESTER UNITED 5–1 FC MIDTJYLLAND

Due to a late injury to Anthony Martial, Marcus was thrown straight into the United starting line-up for this Europa League second leg match. And at the age of eighteen, he took his chance amazingly well. Marcus played the full ninety minutes, scoring two goals and causing all kinds of problems with his speed and movement. A new star was born at Old Trafford.

20 MARCH 2016, MANCHESTER CITY 0–1 MANCHESTER UNITED

Marcus's incredible first month of first-team football continued with this big Manchester derby. City were the team to beat and United did just that, thanks to a great goal from their new young superstar. Marcus used his speed and skill to beat Martín Demichelis and then calmly shoot past Joe Hart. After only eight games, he was already a United hero.

3 JULY 2018, COLOMBIA 1–1 ENGLAND (WON ON PENALTIES!)

Although Marcus only came on for the last seven minutes of this World Cup Round of 16 match, he still played his part. Manager Gareth Southgate needed his coolest, calmest heads for the penalty shoot-out, and Marcus was certainly one of those. With the pressure on, he went second for England, striking the ball confidently into the bottom corner. Ice-cold!

4 6 MARCH 2019,
PSG 1–3 MANCHESTER UNITED

Kylian who? Marcus went head-to-head with Mbappé in the Champions League Round of 16 and came out on the winning side. He gave PSG defender Thilo Kehrer a game to forget, setting one goal up for Romelu Lukaku and then scoring the winner from the penalty spot in the last nail-biting seconds. Once again, Marcus had shown that he was a big game player.

5 30 OCTOBER 2019,
CHELSEA 1–2 MANCHESTER UNITED

On the night before his twenty-second birthday, Marcus proved himself to be United's new star striker. After giving his team the lead with a first-half penalty, he then won the game with a beautiful, swerving free kick from thirty-five yards out. And from that day onwards, Marcus just couldn't stop scoring, reaching nineteen goals by January.

PLAY LIKE YOUR HEROES

THE MARCUS RASHFORD PENALTY ROUTINE

STEP 1: Use your super-speed to race into the opposition box, whether it's you on the ball or one of your teammates. You never know what might happen next…

STEP 2: …PENALTY! As soon as the referee points to the spot, grab the ball and tuck it under your arm. It's yours; don't let anyone take it away from you.

STEP 3: Place it down carefully on the spot, taking a quick look up at the target. Yep, it's still there!

STEP 4: When the referee blows his whistle, take four little shuffles across to the left (that's if you're right-footed, by the way).

STEP 5: Then run forward towards the ball, taking short, stuttering steps to try to fool the keeper.

STEP 6: BANG! Make sure you strike the ball with lots of power, and lots of accuracy too. Aiming for a bottom corner is always best.

STEP 7: GOAL! Keep your celebrations classy and cool, unless, of course, you've just scored a last-minute winner in the Champions League.

TEST YOUR KNOWLEDGE

QUESTIONS

1. Who scored a hat-trick when Marcus went to watch his first-ever Manchester United match?

2. Name at least two other United players who started out at Fletcher Moss Rangers.

3. What did Marcus's brother, Dwaine, do when he first signed for United, aged nine?

4. Marcus used to sneak into the gym to watch which United player practising?

5. Which older United academy players invited Marcus to improve his skills in 'The Cage'?

6. Which Manchester United manager gave Marcus his first team debut?

7. What club trophy did Marcus win at the end of his sensational first season?

8. Marcus played for the England senior team before he played for the Under-21s – true or false?

9. Which three shirt numbers has Marcus worn for Manchester United?

10. Which Manchester United manager helped Marcus to become a better finisher?

11. Which country did Marcus score twice against in the 2018–19 UEFA Nations League?

Answers below. . . No cheating!

1. *The Brazilian Ronaldo (for Real Madrid)* **2.** *Any of Wes Brown, Jesse Lingard, Danny Welbeck and Ravel Morrison* **3.** *He passed his driving test and bought a car so that he could drive Marcus to training!* **4.** *Cristiano Ronaldo* **5.** *Paul Pogba, Jesse Lingard and Ravel Morrison* **6.** *Louis van Gaal* **7.** *The FA Cup* **8.** *True! In the one match he played for the Under-21s after Euro 2016, he scored a hat-trick!* **9.** *39, 19 and 10* **10.** *Ole Gunnar Solskjær* **11.** *Spain*

CAN'T GET ENOUGH OF
ULTIMATE FOOTBALL HEROES?

**Check out heroesfootball.com
for quizzes, games, and competitions!**

**Plus join the Ultimate Football Heroes
Fan Club to score exclusive content
and be the first to hear about new
books and events.
heroesfootball.com/subscribe/**